Supporting children's learning

A training programme for foster carers

Clare Pallet, John Simmonds
and Andrea Warman

BAAF
ADOPTION
& FOSTERING

British Association for Adoption & Fostering
(BAAF)
Saffron House
6–10 Kirby Street
London EC1N 8TS
www.baaf.org.uk

Charity registration 275689 (England and Wales) and SC039337 (Scotland)

British Library Cataloguing in Publication Data
A catalogue record for this book is available from the British Library

ISBN 978 1 905664 15 3

Project management by Shaila Shah, Director of Publications, BAAF

Photograph on cover from www.iStockphoto.com

Designed and typeset by Helen Joubert Design

Printed in Great Britain by The Lavenham Press

Trade distribution by Turnaround Publisher Services, Unit 3, Olympia Trading Estate, Coburg Road, London N22 6TZ

BAAF is the leading UK-wide membership organisation for all those concerned with adoption, fostering and child care issues.

Contents

	The emerging role of carers in facilitating children's learning	i
	Ten frequently asked questions	vi
	How to use this training programme	x
SESSION 1:	**Supporting children's learning**	1
SESSION 2:	**What are the barriers to learning and what can we do about them?**	15
SESSION 3:	**How to work with schools and support children's education**	31
SESSION 4:	**Paired reading: supporting children's literacy**	46
SESSION 5:	**Paired reading practice with the carer and their child**	60
SESSION 6:	**Supporting learning through the use of praise**	62
SESSION 7:	**Supporting self-esteem**	81
SESSION 8:	**Promoting emotional literacy**	101
SESSION 9:	**Listening skills**	125
SESSION 10:	**Pulling it together and moving on**	142

Notes about the authors

Clare Pallett has worked as a social worker in mental health and adoption and fostering. She set up the Fostering Changes training programme with colleagues at the Maudsley Hospital in south London. This is a training programme for carers that develops skills in managing difficult behaviour and promoting positive relationships. The training programme is published by BAAF and is currently being "rolled out" across the country by the Fostering Changes Team at the Maudsley. She currently works with a CAMHS team for looked after children, working with children and their carers.

Dr John Simmonds is Director of Policy, Research and Development at BAAF, and a social worker. He is currently responsible for leading and co-ordinating BAAF's work in health, the law, research, social work and black and minority ethnic issues. He is also currently part of a team researching the long-term impact of adoption on 100 women adopted from Hong Kong in the 1960s, funded by the Nuffield Foundation; and part of another team researching unaccompanied young people in foster care, funded by Big Lottery. Recent publications include 'The making and breaking of relationships – organisational and clinical questions in providing services for looked after children' in *Clinical Child Psychology and Psychiatry* and 'Developing a curiosity about adoption: a psychoanalytical perspective' in Hindle and Shulman (2008) *The Emotional Experience of Adoption: A psychoanalytic perspective.* He also co-edited *The Child Placement Handbook* with Gillian Schofield (published by BAAF in 2009).

Andrea Warman was Fostering Policy, Research and Development Consultant for BAAF till 2009, when she joined the Who Cares? Trust. Andrea began her career as a children and families social worker, going on to train social workers and to lecture and conduct research in social work and social policy at a number of universities. Her most recent publication, *Recipes for Fostering* (BAAF, 2009), looked at the role of food and cooking in helping foster carers to maintain successful placements and build strong bonds with the children they care for. While at BAAF, she also authored *Who am I and what do I do?* in 2007.

Acknowledgements

We would like to thank all the agencies and individuals who have given their time and energy to pilot this training programme in its earlier stages, and who have helped us shape and develop it.

Southwark Children's Services, especially Susan Sinclair
Foster Care Co-Operative and Laurie Gregory
Supported Fostering Services and Alan Fisher
All the foster carers and their children who took part
Professor Keith Topping for his advice and support
Julie Casey, who provided consultation on the SEAL materials
The South London and Maudsley Trust

Thanks are also due to the following for their input and help: Margaret Grant, for conducting the reading exercises with the children, and for administrative support throughout the project; Eileen Fursland, for her valuable help in editing the script; and Roger Harmar, for preparing the material on the CD-ROM. And finally, the heroic efforts of Shaila Shah and Jo Francis, who crafted our work into what appears here.

The mirror writing exercise on page 27 has been reproduced with permission from *Reading and Writing*, by Sian Rees and Foufou Savitzky, published in 2001 by the LLU at South Bank University.

The Feelings Detective posters reproduced on page 114 are Crown Copyright 2005, and were produced by the Department for Education and Skills.

We would also like to thank all those carers and children who appeared in the film, *Paired Reading*, which was directed by Kathy Ryan for Hesketh Crean and produced by Hesketh Crean. Thanks also to Professor Keith Topping who gave us invaluable advice.

This project and training programme have been kindly supported by the following funders:

1E
clore duffield foundation
Esmée Fairbairn Foundation
KPMG FOUNDATION
SHINE
DCSF Innovations Unit

The emerging role of carers in facilitating children's learning

Introduction

Schools, teaching, and learning for all children have never been far from public consciousness and they have always been subject to political, policy and practice debate and controversy. Education is the route to a civilised, successful and prosperous society – one where opportunity and advancement flourish. It is a major preoccupation for most families with a concern about the availability of the "best" school for one's children, their success in the more formal aspects of education such as exams, their achievement in music, art or sport, their general welfare and happiness at school and their success in making and sustaining friendships.

School life and family life are separate arenas in which children develop but they are also linked. Children learn at home and they learn at school. The aspirations, resources and support of parents clearly has a link to the child's aspirations, readiness to learn and capacity to make use of learning opportunities available to them. Schools may frustrate this or they may enhance it. It is possible that, where children have a difficult family life, school provides a source of achievement and positive self-esteem not available to them at home. There are complex two-way relationships between home and school, but at the same time the link between equality and achievement cannot be disputed. A recent report from the Sutton Trust (Washbrook and Waldfogel, 2010) found that those children from the poorest 20 per cent of families are just over 11 months behind in vocabulary scores compared with children from middle-income families. When this gap was explored, parenting style, including sensitivity, setting effective boundaries, parent–child reading and educational visits were shown to account for up to half of the gap. This takes us into familiar territory, where the consequences for families who live in circumstances generated by inequality fall heavily on the opportunities and aspirations of children in those households. It dramatically impacts on their educational attainment and this starts from the point when they are born. It reminds us that it is not sufficient when we think about education and learning to focus only on what happens in school. Learning, achievement and attainment are co-located in family life, school life and the circumstances created by society in the way that it makes opportunity and resources available to children and their families.

Where does education fit in?

It is something of a surprise that, when family life breaks down to such an extent that children become the responsibility of the State, learning and education become rather lost to view. The responsibility and preoccupation with ensuring that the placement is stable and secure and focused on meeting the child's needs is understandable and critically important. But where education and learning fit into this is much less clear.

A number of studies have identified this problem stretching back over 20 years or so. Around that time, Jackson (1987) identified the challenge when she said 'researchers and practitioners do not see education as a particularly interesting or important aspect of care'. At about the same time, one group of researchers (Heath *et al*, 1989) *did* start to explore the issue. In comparing children in care aged 8–14 with children in the general population by using a standardised score for reading, vocabulary and numeracy, 91 per cent of the children in care group were found to have attained a below average score. When another group of children – whose families had received help from social workers but had not been in care – were compared, the results were similarly poor, with 87 per cent of those children scoring below 100. The study also explored emotional and behavioural disorders and estimated 31.4 per cent prevalence for children in foster care and 45.5 per cent for children whose families were receiving help but who were not in care. This compares with Rutter's prevalence rate of 6.8 per cent in the Isle of Wight study (Rutter *et al*, 1970). Other evidence from Heath *et al's* study showed relatively high levels of involvement of foster carers with their children's education and their recreational activities compared with children not in care but where there was social services involvement. Many of the children had been in foster care for a significant time and the study suggested that 'the (experiences of) foster children in the sample is not unlike that of "average" parents with their natural children'. However, the study was also clear that the attainment of these children was 'more typical of those in some of the most disadvantaged home environments'. Questions were raised about the long-term impact of pre-care experiences of abuse and neglect and, very importantly, the impact of inequality for those children living with their parents and receiving social services help.

In a subsequent paper (Aldgate *et al*, 1992), a hypothesis was tested that those children in a planned long-term placement might be in a more settled environment conducive to educational progress – the analysis showed that children who had been performing poorly at the beginning of the study and had come into care because of abuse or neglect made the most progress. This was evidenced in the reading tests and also the vocabulary and maths tests. Overall, the study found that stability of placement – an expectation that the placement would last 'for the duration of childhood' was related to educational progress.

In a further study (Heath *et al*, 1994), there was evidence that receiving special help at school resulted in significant progress on standardised reading scores. There was also evidence of an association between foster carers' own level of educational attainment and the child's reading and vocabulary scores, although children in the most educationally advantaged placements did not show greater progress over the study's timescale. Overall, the conclusion was that, even where there was progress, 'our foster children failed, in general, to demonstrate greater relative progress over the course of our study than the comparison group'. Children's early experience of abuse and neglect were identified as having 'a profound effect on their educational attainment in middle childhood'. Heath *et al* concluded that, when "average" educational inputs are given to children with "above average" educational needs, they fail to make "greater than average" educational progress...Our suggestion is that 'greater-than-average progress needs greater-than average inputs'.

These conclusions are clear – it is not a message of despair but one where a clear understanding of the origins of the disadvantages that children bring with them into foster care and into school are addressed through 'high quality, compensatory experience from social workers, carers and schools' (Berridge and Saunders, 2009).

The role of foster carers

The role of foster carers in learning, education and schools has often not been very explicit. Many of the studies on outcomes, including Cheesbrough's (2002) analysis of the 1970 British Cohort Study, show that, for children in foster care, their educational progress at best has been similar to those of children from a similar socio-economic background. That analysis concludes that 'much of the future attainment of the child could be identified in educational test scores at age 5...very early progress at school can be a protective factor if it brings encouragement from teachers and carers...this analysis shows the importance of very early interventions to give some of the most disadvantaged children, who may enter care at a very young age, a better start in their educational careers' (p 51).

The last Labour government, from very early on in their administration, set a number of programmes in train to identify how policy and practice might develop to address the issues. It is important to acknowledge the wide span of programmes to address this issue, with stability of placements, effective planning and decision making as core. Health and education were built into this by establishing key roles such as designated teachers and health professionals and, in time, virtual head teachers. A recognition of the significance of behavioural difficulties and their impact on placements was also key to policy and practice development with *Fostering Changes* (Pallett *et al,* 2005) being developed to specifically help foster carers effectively manage emotional and behavioural difficulties in children. Other programmes that had become well established as evidence-based practice in the USA, such as multi-dimensional treatment foster care, were piloted to explore the relevance of programmes.

Foster carers were clearly seen to have a critical role in education and learning but little was available beyond that which individual fostering providers managed to establish. The question of the foster carer's specific role in relation to school, education and learning was not clarified and could therefore be left to chance. Is it the role of the social worker to talk to teachers or attend parent evenings or liaise with school where important decisions need to be made? Does the foster carer primarily have a supportive role in relation to a child's learning – ensuring they go to school with the right equipment and that they have the resources, space and time to complete homework tasks? Or should they play an active role in taking a direct interest in what the child is learning and facilitating and enhancing this? And what do they do if the child is struggling because they are unmotivated or have emotional and behavioural challenges? Is this then for the social worker to sort out with the school and the SENCO or designated teacher or does the carer have a more direct role? The answers to these questions will depend on individual circumstances – the child, their circumstances, the placement purpose and objectives, the fostering provider and many other issues. But as a general principle and consistent with many developments in foster care over recent years, the foster carer does have a core role supportive of the view expressed above that 'greater-than-average progress needs greater-than average inputs'.

Supporting Children's Learning training programme

It is this principle that has driven the development of this training programme. The foster carer is seen to have a primary role in engaging with the child in supporting their learning. This is explored generally by identifying what enables and supports engagement in learning with a key issue being the relationship between the carer and the child. A sensitive, interested and supportive relationship, which gives a child the space and time to learn, and where they are motivated, interested and enthused and receive positive and appropriate feedback is explored throughout the programme. Many aspects of this will be recognisable in what makes for the development of secure attachments. However, while a secure attachment relationship may facilitate learning, it is not a necessary pre-requisite. But the programme recognises that, for both children and adults, how we feel about ourselves as people and as learners, the development of positive self-esteem, and the engagement and availability of feedback from trusted people is both generally and specifically facilitative of learning. The use of such principles is also recognisable in many parenting programmes such as those by Webster Stratton and, in particular, the *Fostering Changes* programme. This latter has very close links with the programme described here. Many of the principles of *Fostering Changes*, which focus on emotional and behavioural difficulties in children in foster care, will also be found here.

The relationship with the foster carer and the foster care "home" environment are key to effective learning and the application of a set of sensitively applied "techniques" support this. The experiences of the foster carer – both positive and negative – in their learning and education are seen to enhance the learning environment or in some situations restrict it. Effective "parenting" is easier to establish when there have been positive, secure and thoughtful experiences in one's own childhood. Engaging positively in learning experiences and doing well in education is helped enormously when parents are confident learners themselves and have experienced success. But where this has not been the case, and while they may make the parenting or learning pathway more of a struggle, it is the capacity to reflect on those experiences and build something out of them that is key. Anxiety, guilt and shame act as impediments to emotional growth and they can act as impediments to learning as well. Understanding how they are expressed in thought and behaviour and how they act as barriers to effectively engaging in learning is key to the course.

Supporting Children's Learning aims to create a group-based learning environment that:

- supports foster carers in reflecting on some of their own learning experiences in order to deepen their understanding of the learning issues that may be faced by the children they are caring for;
- identifies a small number of techniques for positively reinforcing their own and the child's experience and engagement in learning;
- reinforces the view that learning can be fun, exciting and rewarding even if sometimes it is a struggle (for almost everyone); and
- explores the relationship between learning, emotions and behaviour.

In addition to an exploration of these objectives, the programme focuses specifically on the development of reading skills. It is very difficult to learn without being able to read; it is also very difficult to become independent without being able to read. The foundations of reading are established from a very young age and although the acquisition of reading skills become more explicit in the school years, early development is still vitally important. Literacy is a major focus in schools and some aspects of this are hotly debated with different approaches being vigorously advocated. This programme has adopted a well-established reading scheme called Paired Reading. There is a clear evidence base for its effectiveness, which is widely accepted. It is of particular value for non-specialists such as parents and it has proved itself with disadvantaged socio-economic groups across the world.

Paired reading enables carers to:

- acquire techniques for supporting and developing a child's reading skills which are non-technical and straightforward to acquire and can be readily modified to accommodate the child's current level of reading development;
- develop their relationship with the child through a shared activity where the carer takes a positive and supportive role; and
- address any difficulties the child encounters by using the techniques specifically developed for paired reading or where the learning issues are more general, by the techniques acquired throughout the programme.

The programme requires fostering providers to do the following.

- To identify as a priority the need to support and train their foster carers to take a proactive role in children's learning and education.
- Identify trainers who are familiar with working with groups of foster carers.
- Provide the trainers with time and support in the planning, delivery and completion of the programme, including familiarisation with the background issues and materials relevant to the programme.

Directly caring for children separated from their parents couldn't be more important. It is a challenging task that demands much but where the rewards couldn't be greater. Completing this course and putting into practice what has been learnt from it can make an enormous difference to the confidence, understanding and skills of carers in directly supporting and enabling children's learning. It contributes to that by placing learning within the context of emotional and behavioural development and the qualities of the relationship between carer and child. While there are challenging issues to be faced, the development team firmly believes that this is within the capabilities of every carer. It builds on what has been learnt since the early identification of the problem in Sonia Jackson's paper. It looks forward to the future when every child has been given the opportunity to grow, develop and learn to their maximum potential. That is the vision for foster care and this course.

Ten frequently asked questions

1 **Is the programme suitable for all foster carers?**

The programme has been designed for foster carers who care for children aged between 5 and 11. The duration of the course requires that the foster carer has the child placed with them for at least 10 weeks and, for the investment to be worthwhile, there should be an expectation that the placement is planned to last for three months or more – both for a settling in phase and a moving in phase to be accommodated if this is the plan. There are no specific prerequisites for the foster carers themselves, although it would usually be expected that they have established themselves in role, i.e. completed basic training requirements for the core role of foster carer. Beyond that, the pilots suggest that the programme is relevant and effective, however much experience the foster carer has.

It may be found that foster carers who have completed the *Fostering Changes* training programme will be particularly ready to make use of this programme.

2 **Do the trainers need to be experienced in teaching or education?**

No. The programme is designed to be used by and relevant to non-specialists in teaching and learning. This is so with regards to both the emotional and behavioural issues in relation to learning as well as the specific literacy programme. However, there may be some issues that do not work according to plan. In such instances, the trainers should have access to appropriate support and consultancy.

3 **Do foster carers need to be educated to a particular level in order to participate?**

Foster carers will be approved taking into account their capacity to meet the requirements as set out in regulation and guidance and put into practice locally. There are no educational requirements specified, although foster carers will be expected to demonstrate their capacity to develop their skills and knowledge in a number of areas and have the motivation and commitment to do so. Foster carers vary enormously in their learning and educational experiences and each brings the fruits of that to bear as a foster carer. The course has been piloted with foster carers from across this spectrum and this includes some carers whose experiences of formal education have been difficult and where their formal attainment levels have been restricted. Where a foster carer has struggled with their own literacy and is lacking in confidence, the course in general will be helpful to them when they experience trainers and a group that are supportive (of which the programme is designed to provide ample opportunity for). Where the child's attainment levels may challenge the foster carer in terms of literacy levels (as they may do where the foster carer has English as a second language), the foster carer may be able to recruit other family members to specifically undertake paired reading. In the process, the carer may find their own confidence will increase or they may address their own issues through other routes (and should be supported to do so).

4 **Do the foster carers in the group all need to be at the same level of educational attainment?**

No. The programme has been piloted with foster carers who were diverse in their educational attainment in many different ways. The key to making this programme work is in the sensitivity and openness of the trainers in the way they work with the group. A part of this is also the sensitivity of the foster carers to each other. The first session provides an opportunity to agree ground rules for the group and this means acknowledging the significance of diversity and difference in the group. The issue will need to be re-visited throughout the programme and everybody will need to be sensitive to it. It may be helpful to remember that this is indicative of the issues children face in the classroom and can be significantly upsetting if not supported properly and sensitively.

5 Is the programme suitable for children of all abilities between 5 and 11?

Broadly, yes. The programme is designed to help carers think about the child's expectations, experiences, motivation and blocks to learning. It recognises that emotional and behavioural issues may act as a barrier to facilitating engagement and encourage motivation. The pilots demonstrated that this happened with very few exceptions and most children moved on from where they were.

Some children may have levels of behavioural and emotional difficulties where the focus of the placement is primarily on managing these. Where this is so, the foster carer and supervising social worker should discuss this and make a decision on delaying the use of the programme to an appropriate time. However, it should be remembered that the programme is intended to be an intervention that may prompt a cycle of positive improvements.

The programme has not been explicitly piloted with children with specific impairments. Children with visual and hearing impairments may well benefit from the programme with the use of appropriate communication technologies. Children with mild to moderate learning difficulties may also benefit significantly. The principle should be one of inclusivity but some thought will need to be given to ensuring that both foster carers and child are properly prepared and supported.

Where English is the child's second language, individual decisions will need to be made about the appropriateness of the use of paired reading. However, for many children it will be an excellent opportunity to facilitate their further acquisition of English.

6 Should the school be informed that the child is taking part in this programme?

Yes. The foster carer should discuss their participation in the programme and identify that they are developing their skills in using paired reading. Many teachers will know of the programme and some may even have used it themselves. The child will also be developing their literacy levels at school and there is no evidence that programmes/approaches in use by the school will conflict with the use of paired reading by the foster carer. If in England, the teacher may want to brief/discuss this with the school's SENCO and the designated teacher for looked after children. The work with the child and their progress should be formally recorded in the relevant education plan for the child.

7 Is it necessary to complete the whole 10 weeks?

The programme has been designed and piloted as a whole. While paired reading has been developed as a stand alone programme elsewhere and can be used as such, the advantage of the whole 10-week programme is that it integrates issues of emotional and behavioural challenges with a positive, evidence-based literacy programme. It also provides essential group-based support to foster carers and facilitates their development. The advantages of this cannot be underestimated.

8 Can the programme be completed on an individual basis or in smaller groups?

Preferably not. The group provides a strong supportive environment to enable the objectives of the programme to be achieved. Reading this manual by itself will be helpful but it cannot enable the kinds of learning experiences that a group-based experience provides. Foster carers often work alone in their home and family so the advantages of bringing them together for programmes like this cannot be underestimated.

For a group to work effectively, it needs to be between 8 and 12 people. It is likely there will be absences from the group from week to week given the pressures of foster care. In order to provide enough continuity for the group to work week to week, there need to be enough members to allow for absences.

9 Can paired reading be learnt without completing the rest of the programme?

Yes, it can, and this is commonly so in many other projects. But as identified above, there are very strong and persuasive reasons for setting it with the context of a group-based activity which focuses on a range of core issues about children in foster care.

10 What is the evidence that the programme is effective?

The literature is extensive, but the following will be found to be helpful.

Aldgate, J., Colton, M., Ghate, D., & Heath, A. (1992) 'Educational attainment and stability in long-term foster care', *Children and Society*, 6:2, pp 91-103

Berridge, D., and Saunders, H. (2009) 'The education of fostered and adopted children', in G. Schofield and J. Simmonds (eds), *The Child Placement Handbook*, London: BAAF, pp 327-344

Cheesbrough, S. (2002) *The Educational Attainment of People who have been in Care: Findings from the 1970 British Cohort Study*, London: London School of Economics

Heath, A., Colton, M., and Aldgate, J. (1989) 'The educational progress of children in and out of care', *British Journal of Social Work*, 19, pp 447-460

Heath, A., Colton, M., and Aldgate, J. (1994) 'Failure to escape: a longitudinal study of foster children's educational attainment', *British Journal of Social Work*, 24, pp 241-260

Jackson, S. (1987) *The Education of Children in Care* Bristol Papers in Applied Social Studies (Vol 3) Bristol: Bristol University.

Pallett, P., Blackeby, K., Yule, W., Weissman, R, W., and Scott, S. (2005) *Fostering Changes: How to improve relationships and manage difficult behaviour*, London: BAAF

Rutter, M., Tizard, J., and Whitmore, K. (1970) *Education, Health and Behaviour*, London: Longman

Topping, K. (1987) 'Paired reading: a powerful technique for parent use', *The Reading Teacher*, 40:7, pp 608-614

Topping, K., and Wolfendale, S. (1995) 'The effectiveness of family literacy programmes', *Reading*, 29:3, p 26

Topping, K. J., and Lindsay, G. A. (1992) 'Paired reading: a review of the literature', *Research Papers in Education*, 7:3, p 199

Washbrook, E., and Waldfogel, J. (2010) *Cognitive Gaps in the Early Years,* London: The Sutton Trust.

How to use this training programme

What this course will do

Supporting Children's Learning has been designed to help carers support the education of children in their care, and to explore how they can enable them to become more confident and effective learners. Support with literacy is a central aspect of the training programme.

Why this course is important

Education is immensely important, yet for looked after children there are a whole range of factors which can create barriers to educational success and which limit life chances. Many carers are eager for their children to experience success at school but they may feel powerless to bring about changes in their child's motivation and interest in school work, or in their behaviour at school.

This course aims to help carers:

- understand the processes involved in learning;
- learn how they can try to create an environment in their home which is conducive to learning;
- support and encourage the development of social and emotional skills which underpin our abilities to learn;
- develop their understanding of the education system and their role within this; and
- learn how they can support their children's literacy skills.

This course takes a broad view of learning. It brings together support for literacy with a focus on the development of "skills for life". In order to succeed in school, children need a range of social and emotional skills which will enable them to access learning and to develop a sense of self-efficacy and self-esteem. Carers are ideally placed to support children with their learning and to help them develop positive attitudes, skills and behaviours which will support them in the school learning environment.

How to use these training materials

The course works best with groups of between 8 and 12 participants.

The course consists of 10 sessions. Each of these lasts four hours, apart from Session 5 which is a paired reading practice session, where trainers observe carers reading with their child. There are a number of different options for organising this session which are outlined in the notes for this session.

Learning is most effective when participants can actively engage with the issues and ideas and share thoughts and experiences with each other. The training materials have been designed and organised to try to encourage participants' active involvement in thinking and working together. The exercises and discussions are an integral part of the learning and carers will value the opportunity of sharing and learning from each other.

What this pack includes

This pack consists of:

- **A CD-ROM containing a PowerPoint slide presentation for each of the sessions and a set of handouts**. The handouts may be printed out and photocopied for distribution to participants attending the course; they may not be used for other purposes and BAAF retains the copyright unless otherwise indicated.
- **A DVD, *Paired Reading.***
- **This book**, which contains the following:

  – reproductions of the PowerPoint presentation for each of the sessions (each presentation includes the aims of that session and all the handouts);

  – suggested training exercises, usually for small group work, to encourage participants to share their thoughts, ideas and experiences and to encourage reflection and learning;

  – suggested discussion questions which the trainer can raise with the group, briefly and informally, at certain points in the presentation.

What you will need

- A flipchart with paper
- A laptop computer with CD-ROM and DVD drives and PowerPoint
- A screen for displaying PowerPoint slides
- Pens, pencils, post-it notes and coloured crayons for participants to use
- Name labels or badges for participants
- Certain sessions require the use of appropriate children's reading material, basic art materials such as glitter and coloured paper, or cards to be prepared from the materials on the CD-ROM.
- Refreshments

Venue

Ideally, this course should be held in a venue that is well-heated, well-lit and comfortable, and that feels welcoming. You will need adequate seating for participants and access to tables will be helpful. You will probably want somewhere that provides refreshments or that has provision for making drinks. If you are presenting this course in full-day sessions, you will also need somewhere which provides lunch or which provides opportunities for participants to buy lunch, or bring lunch with them and eat it in the venue. You will need to think about whether your venue is easily accessible to carers. Is it on good transport routes? Is there disabled access? Parking? Is there a crèche?

Evaluation

On the CD-ROM, an evaluation form is provided for participants to complete and return. This is important for the course leaders, your organisation and the carers themselves. Evaluation allows the service users to voice their opinions of the training, and contribute to improvements in its provision, and it provides you and your organisation with invaluable feedback about the impact and effectiveness of what you do.

How to run training groups

Preparation

The course is best run by two co-workers. Trainers may want to consider recruiting a carer from their authority or agency who has a special interest or experience in education, who might work with them. It is important that one of the trainers has experience in working with foster carers and/or looked after children. Agencies should ensure that course leaders:

- have the necessary training skills;
- have an understanding of adult learning principles;
- are committed to anti-discriminatory practice;
- are familiar with the course content and are confident in delivering this.

Trainers will need to familiarise themselves with the paired reading approach before they start the training. This is not difficult, but it will require that they practise the skills. This can be done initially in role-play with a colleague; however, trainers will need to practise with a child, ideally one who is not yet a perfect reader. Trainers will soon pick up the skills, and gain an experience of the challenges and the benefits of this approach.

Creating a safe and stimulating environment for learning

Most adults and children learn best when they feel safe, relaxed and comfortable. It is therefore part of the trainers' responsibility to try to facilitate the development of trust within the group and to create an environment that is open, engaging and fun, and where it is safe to make mistakes and acknowledge shortcomings.

The trainers' role is to facilitate the group process and to encourage everyone to engage with the learning and to contribute their personal ideas, understanding and experience. Trainers need to ensure that particular individuals do not dominate discussion, and that those who are quieter are given the necessary support and opportunities to contribute what they would wish to.

Learning needs to be relevant and engaging in order to maintain participants' attention and involvement. You will need to be sensitive to the learning style of your group members, and think about how you can use visual, auditory and kinaesthetic cues to stimulate learning. It is also good modelling to be aware of other needs within the group, for example, the need for food or drink; the right temperature or level of activity; and so on. There may be times when you feel you need to vary the pace or style of training in order to create a change in mood or energy in the group. It can be useful to have a few brief, active and fun activities up your sleeve to energise the group, and to facilitate the transition from one activity to another.

We have found that the subject of "education", and the associated ideas of "success" and "achievement" have been emotive ones. For this reason, trainers will need to be sensitive to themes that emerge in the process of training, and voice any concerns and anxieties that arise in connection with this. Many of the carers who have attended our course have had difficult and sometimes traumatic experiences of learning and education. It has been important to acknowledge these experiences and the impact that they have had. On occasions, this has been a positive and powerful experience, and has enabled some carers to re-evaluate their experiences and feelings about themselves and develop a more positive sense of self.

Another vital aspect of the training experience has been the importance of creating a positive environment where carers can take pride in their achievements, talents and their commitment to their role and to their children. Supporting carers to recognise personal qualities and skills is an important part of developing their sense of confidence and self-efficacy. Positive attitudes and aspirations are key to motivation and success and so it is important that trainers model affirming and "can-do" attitudes and qualities.

Diversity issues

It is your responsibility to ensure that the course is accessible to everyone and that all participants – whatever their ethnic background, sexuality or educational level – feel equally valued, respected and able to contribute. As a trainer, you need to be sensitive to the composition of the group and consider how you will include and address the needs of participants who are from minority ethnic groups, who have a disability, who are single or gay or lesbian.

If any participants have disabilities, check the accessibility of the building, the layout of the room and any communications aids. And if necessary, make sure a parking space will be available for participants with mobility difficulties, close to the building. Asking participants in advance about any disabilities will forewarn you about the need for a British Sign Language interpreter or the need to provide handouts in a larger type size, for instance.

When setting dates for training, be careful not to clash with any religious holidays.

SESSION 1: Supporting children's learning

TIMETABLE

Section	Timing	Materials
1. Welcome and introduction	**10.00–10.10**	Name badges/labels, folders containing handouts Slide
2. Starter: getting to know each other Aims of the session	**10.10–10.30**	Starter sheet (on CD-ROM) Slide
3. Exercise: 'What I hope to get from the course'	**10.30–10.45**	Flip chart
4. Overview of training: what we will learn about	**10.45–10.55**	Slide Handout 1.1: *Overview of the programme*
5. Ground rules: 'What I need from this group is...'	**10.55–11.20**	Flip chart
6. Discussion: what do we mean by "learning" and "education"?	**11.20–11.35**	Flip chart
7. Pairs exercise: reflecting on our own experience	**11.35–12.05**	
8. Break	**12.05–12.25**	Refreshments
9. Group exercise: what skills do children need to do well at school? Group reflection	**12.25–12.55**	Blank post-it notes, pens and flip chart
10. Introduction to the social and emotional aspects of learning Exercise: what are social and emotional skills?	**12.55–1.25**	Slide Handout 1.2 *The social and emotional aspects of learning* Prepared post-it notes and flip chart
11. Personal reflection: achievement shield	**1.25–1.35**	Handout 1.3 *Achievement shield*
12. Home practice	**1.35–1.45**	Handout 1.4 *Celebration shield*
13. Evaluation	**1.45–1.55**	Sample *Evaluation form*
14. Closing round	**1.55–2.00**	

PREPARATION

- Prepare the room and set out the chairs and any tables so as to facilitate group discussion.
- Have files or folders containing handouts for today's session ready to give to carers as they arrive. These will be used throughout the course.
- Set up your laptop and projector ready for use.
- Prepare the flip chart ready for some of the activities.
- Make arrangements for any drinks and refreshments that you need.

Welcome each carer as they arrive – you may want to provide labels or badges for carers to write their names on.

RESOURCES

Files for carers
Name labels or badges
Flip chart, pens
Laptop, CD-ROM with Powerpoint presentation, projector, screen (if necessary)
Post-it notes prepared for exercises
Blank post-it notes
Refreshments

HANDOUTS

Please print these from the CD-ROM supplied and give each carer a copy of the handouts for today.

Starter – getting to know one another
1.1 *Overview of the programme*
1.2 *The social and emotional aspects of learning*
1.3 *Achievement shield*
1.4 *Celebration shield*
Evaluation

10 minutes

WELCOME AND INTRODUCTION

You will need to:

- welcome the group
- introduce yourselves as trainers
- inform the group of any health and safety procedures
- make sure carers know where the toilets are

Introduce the course by saying that:

THE FOSTERING EDUCATION PROJECT – SUPPORTING CHILDRENS' LEARNING

- has been tested and developed with both local authority and independent foster care providers
- combines fun, some hard work and lots of interesting ideas and materials
- enables everybody to have opportunities to share experiences and skills and to develop their learning and understanding together

20 minutes

STARTER

Getting to know each other

Ask carers to find their starter sheet, which will be in their folder – the sheet is supplied on the CD-ROM. Ask them to get up and go around the group and find someone who fits each of the ten statements on the sheet and to write their names in the appropriate boxes.

Reconvene the group and ask carers to introduce themselves using a statement from the sheet. Model this by introducing yourself briefly. For example: 'My name is Maxine and as a child I loved school dinners!'

Introduce the aims of today's session.

AIMS OF TODAY'S SESSION:

- Enable carers to get to know each other and to find out about the course
- Explore and clarify the aims of training
- Define what we mean by the terms "education" and "learning"
- Explore what skills children need to become effective and confident learners

15 minutes

EXERCISE

What I hope to get from the course

Carers may have come to training with some specific hopes and expectations and so it is useful to find out about what they hope to learn or achieve. Give everybody an opportunity to voice what they hope to get out of the training and write this on the flip chart.

Note for trainers: If group members bring up issues that radically depart from the course structure and content, you will need to think about whether you can accommodate these or not. You may need to help participants think about where to find support to address their particular questions or needs.

10 minutes

OVERVIEW OF TRAINING

What we will learn about

Explain to the carers that the aim of the course is to help develop their understanding and skills so that they can support their children in becoming more confident and motivated learners. The following slide shows the major components covered in the course.

OVERVIEW OF TRAINING

- Understanding learning
- Creating a space to learn
- Skills that underlie learning
- Understanding the education system
- Supporting literacy

Refer carers to Handout 1.1, *Overview of the programme*, for more details on what will be covered.

25 minutes

GROUND RULES

'What I need from this group is...'

Ask carers, in pairs, to think about their experiences in previous groups and to recall one that was positive and comfortable for them and one that was not. Ask them to try and identify what contributed to this.

Reconvene in the large group and find out from each carer one thing they need to make the group positive and safe for them. Write this up on the flip chart, discussing and clarifying each item with the group. You, as trainers, can contribute to this process as well. Make sure that issues relating to confidentiality, safeguarding and diversity are covered. (Starting and finishing times and mobile phone use are two other favourites.)

At the end of the discussion there should be a workable set of rules that act as a good starting point. You may need to refer to these throughout the course and add to or modify them as necessary. Creating a good atmosphere conducive to learning is an active and ongoing process and should not be confined to the beginning of a course.

15 minutes

DISCUSSION

What do we mean by "learning" and "education"? Are they the same or are they different?

On the flip chart write up the words "learning" and "education". Ask carers to call out what they think each term means, using examples if that is helpful.

Note for trainers: There are no "right" answers here! The group may have all sorts of different ideas, which may include some of the following.

Education may be seen as having the following features:

- more formal and organised
- usually happens within a particular place or context – a school or class
- the content is often specific and structured
- it is imparted from one person or source to another

Learning may be seen as:

- a life-long process which occurs both in and out of school
- more informal, including experiences in the home, with friends, in sporting activities, at clubs and so on
- something that the child may take greater ownership of and which they enjoy
- something that can happen through observing others' actions and example or doing things together
- something that can happen without our being aware of it

Children are learning all the time and most of that learning (estimated at around 85%) occurs outside formal education. Carers have a central role in helping children learn and develop a range of skills for life.

30 minutes

PAIRS EXERCISE

Reflecting on our own experience of school and education

Explain to the group that it is helpful to understand and be aware of our own feelings and experiences. This exercise is designed to help carers get in touch with their own early experiences of school – perhaps their first day at school or other significant memories.

Divide the group into pairs and ask them to recall some of their memories. Acknowledge that some carers may have had difficult experiences and reassure them that they need only share what they want to. Allow carers sufficient time for an exchange of experiences and then invite them to feed back to the group.

Note for trainers: This exercise needs to be handled with sensitivity. Many carers have found this exercise a powerful one and it has made them more aware of how their own experiences of schooling continue to resonate in their lives. It can be instructive for the group to take stock of the differences in their school experiences and to learn from each other.

20 minutes

BREAK

30 minutes

GROUP EXERCISE

What skills do children need to do well at school?

What are the skills that children need in order to learn well and get on with others at school? In two small groups, ask carers to identify skills and to write each one on a post-it note. One group is to focus on the classroom setting and the other group should think about informal settings such as the playground. Encourage carers to think broadly about the variety of skills children need, including social and personal skills as well as more academic ones. Ask carers to describe these as specifically as they can. You may want to give a couple of examples from the list as prompts.

Prepare a flip chart with two headings: "Personal and life skills" and "Academic and subject skills". Ask each group to take turns to place each post-it note on the flip chart, discussing whether the skill falls more under one heading than another.

Examples of skills that children need to be successful in school:

PERSONAL AND LIFE SKILLS

- sitting quietly
- listening to others
- following instructions
- co-operating
- keeping calm and positive
- drawing skills

ACADEMIC AND SUBJECT SKILLS

- skills with numbers
- wide vocabulary
- literacy skills
- general knowledge

- taking turns
- organisational skills
- asking for help and support

Point out to the group that some degree of emotional and social skills underpins every task that children are asked to complete, both at school and elsewhere.

Group reflection

Ask carers to reflect on the kinds of social and emotional skills that they had to use in the last task and to share this in the group.

Examples might include: listening, taking turns, smiling and nodding, seeking common ground, being polite, asking clarifying questions, not dominating, encouraging, etc.

It may be helpful to acknowledge how emotionally powerful and anxiety-provoking new learning situations can be. Ask if anyone is able to share a feeling that they have experienced today in relation to attending the training – this might be, for example, anxiety about getting something "wrong" or embarrassment about not knowing or understanding something.

Note for trainers: Discomfort at new learning situations can be extreme. One carer acknowledged that she'd felt like running from the room as she feared that she might make a fool of herself if she'd misunderstood instructions. It is helpful for us as adults to keep in touch with how frightening and confusing learning situations can be, so that we can better empathise with our children's experiences.

30 minutes

INTRODUCTION TO THE SOCIAL AND EMOTIONAL ASPECTS OF LEARNING

Explain to the carers that today's observations and discussions make it clear that learning is not just an intellectual activity but that it relies on a broad range of social and emotional skills. Absence of these skills affects children's abilities to cope with a whole host of different everyday situations and affects how they feel and think about themselves as learners.

THE SOCIAL AND EMOTIONAL ASPECTS OF LEARNING
In order to learn, children need:

- Emotional skills – to know and understand themselves
  – to manage their feelings
- Social skills – to form and negotiate relationships with others

Children who can manage their feelings and who are able to form and negotiate relationships are more likely to become motivated and successful learners.

THE FIVE COMPONENTS OF SOCIAL AND EMOTIONAL LEARNING ARE:

- self-awareness
- managing feelings
- motivation
- empathy
- social skills

The social and emotional aspects of learning can be broken down into these five components. Over the course of the training, we shall be exploring how carers can support their children in each of these areas. Tell the carers that more information about this can be found on Handout 1.2, *The social and emotional aspects of learning*, in their folders.

Note for trainers: The former Department for Children, Schools and Families (DCSF) developed a wide range of resources for school settings, which are designed to build the necessary social and emotional skills that children need to become confident, enthusiastic and effective learners. Some children will be familiar with SEAL (Social and Emotional Aspects of Learning) ideas and skills through input from their schools. See: www.nationalstrategies.standards.dcsf.gov.uk/node/87009.

EXERCISE

What are social and emotional skills?

This exercise provides carers with an opportunity to explore what "social and emotional skills" might actually look like in everyday situations.

Divide the group into two smaller groups. Give each group a flip chart sheet and ask them to write the five components of social and emotional learning as headings on the sheet. You will need to have prepared (in duplicate) post-it notes with some of the following skills and abilities written on them.

Knowing how you learn best ◆ knowing what you are good/not good at ◆ knowing how you come across to other people ◆ controlling your anger ◆ managing boredom ◆ calming yourself when upset ◆ recognising your own feelings ◆ tolerating criticism ◆ knowing how to express your feelings without hurting others ◆ stopping to think before you act ◆ ability to concentrate ◆ ability to work towards goals ◆ persistence ◆ working independently ◆ organisational skills ◆ negotiation skills ◆ ability to bounce back after setbacks ◆ seeing events from another's point of view ◆ anticipating others' reactions ◆ realising your behaviour can make others feel better or worse ◆ understanding that people express themselves in different ways ◆ valuing differences ◆ assertiveness skills ◆ understanding what makes and breaks relationships ◆ ability to communicate with different groups/audiences ◆ ability to work towards resolving differences ◆ co-operation

In their small group, ask each carer to take a few post-it notes and, in turn, to place each one in the category that seems most appropriate, explaining to the group their reasoning. Some behaviours and abilities may straddle more than one category and carers should decide where they think it best fits. Provide support and clarification to the groups as necessary.

At the end of this exercise, ask carers to feed back to the large group.

10 minutes

PERSONAL REFLECTION

Achievement shield

Ask carers to find their copy of Handout 1.3, *Achievement shield,* in their folder. Explain to the group that acknowledging our achievements can have a positive impact on how we feel about ourselves and on our attitude towards learning. Over the coming weeks, we hope that carers will get in touch with some of their own talents and achievements. To start this off today, ask carers to write in the right-hand top segment of their personal achievement shield something they are proud of. This may relate to fostering or it may be something completely different. Allow a few minutes to do this. Explain that you will return to the achievement shield at the end of the session.

10 minutes

HOME PRACTICE

Celebration shield

Carers will also have a copy of Handout 1.4, *Celebration shield,* in their folders. The idea of the celebration shield is to acknowledge and celebrate their child's positive qualities and the things the child is good at and enjoys. Explain that you would like them to work on this with their child in the intervening week.

Success at school is partly dependent upon confidence and having a positive image of oneself as a learner. Explain to the carers that this week you want them to spend some time with their child, talking with them about the things the child is good at and enjoys doing. Encourage carers to think broadly about social skills, interests and hobbies, academic and practical skills and talents. Encourage them to be specific and to make as long a list as they can!

Examples might include: reading, keeping their bedroom tidy, drawing, football, telling jokes, listening carefully, computer games, sharing toys, baking, basketball, following instructions, looking after pets, being polite, being good at talking, going to the park, having a friendly smile, going to Scouts and other clubs, singing nicely, dancing and so on.

Carers should encourage their child to write or draw and to fill in the Celebration shield in whatever way the child feels comfortable with. It is important to make this a fun exercise and to encourage creativity. **Ask the carers to bring the completed shield back next week to share with the group.**

10 minutes

EVALUATION

Give each carer a session evaluation form (available on the CD-ROM) to complete and explain that there will be a brief evaluation after each session.

5 minutes

CLOSING ROUND

At times we find it hard to be positive about our own abilities and skills and so it is important to remind ourselves about our talents, skills and achievements. Ask carers to share with the rest of the group one thing that they wrote down on their achievement shield – something they are proud of.

HANDOUT 1.1

Overview of the programme

Supporting literacy
- paired reading
- pre-reading skills

Understanding the education system
- understanding the jargon
- clarifying carer's role

Skills that underlie learning: social and emotional skills
- self-esteem
- motivation
- self-awareness
- managing feelings

Creating a space to learn
- creating learning routines
- providing a stimulating home environment
- using praise and encouragement

Understanding learning
- empathy with new learners
- learning styles
- barriers to learning

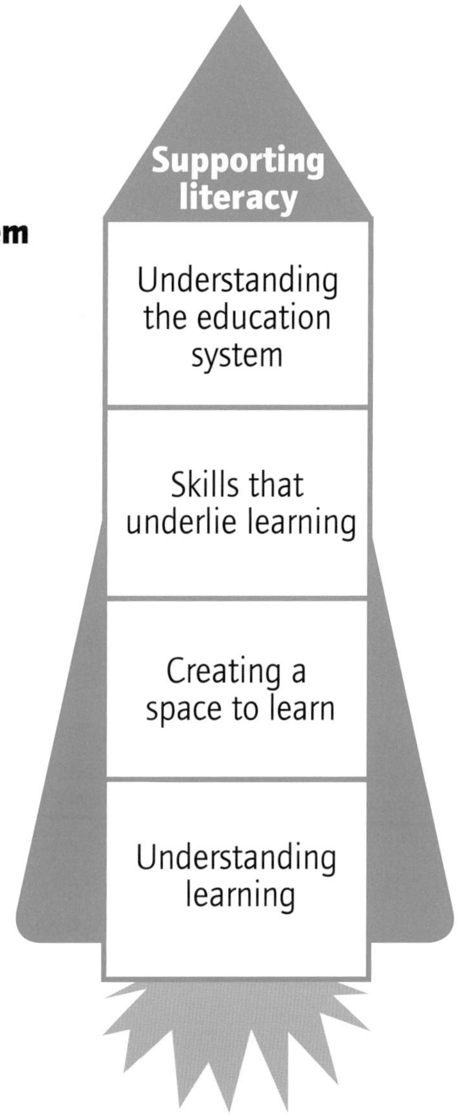

HANDOUT 1.2

The social and emotional aspects of learning

Children do not learn in a vacuum – they learn from the people around them and from their surroundings. So you could say that learning is, at its core, a social process. In order to learn successfully, children need to have a whole variety of different personal and interpersonal skills in place. There is increasing interest in what is often referred to as "emotional intelligence" or the "social and emotional aspects of learning".

In order to be successful at school, children don't just need to be able to read, write and know their numbers. They will also need to have learned a variety of life skills, such as the ability to:

- defer gratification
- take responsibility for their actions
- deal with peer pressure
- feel positively about themselves
- make and sustain relationships... and so on.

These skills are some of the basic building blocks for getting on in life. They are often considered to fall into two main categories – the personal and the interpersonal.

- The **personal** covers areas of learning that enable us to know and understand ourselves – to identify our feelings, to know our strengths and weaknesses and to recognise what motivates us. It is this kind of understanding that enables us to manage our feelings, take responsibility for our behaviour and keep going in the face of setbacks.
- The **interpersonal** skills, in contrast, enable us to form social relationships – to co-operate, solve problems, resolve conflicts and enjoy and respect differences between people as well as similarities. The key skill in this area is empathy – the ability to understand others.

These skills underlie almost every aspect of school, home and community life, including how to learn effectively and get on with other people.

The social and emotional skills that contribute to our ability to learn are often grouped under the following five broad headings:

- self-awareness
- managing feelings
- motivation
- empathy
- social skills

KEY SKILLS

Self-awareness

This involves knowing yourself, for example, how you learn best and how you relate to others. It also involves knowing about how you think and feel. Children who are self-aware are more able to organise themselves and plan their learning. These skills help them to take responsibility for their actions, to feel good about the things they do well, to recognise when they find things hard and to accept themselves for who they are.

Managing feelings

When children can recognise and accept their feelings, they can start to manage or "regulate" them more appropriately. In learning situations, they can use these skills to calm themselves and to manage worry and frustration. As children learn how to manage feelings, they learn that the way they express feelings affects others. They may also learn how to look after their own needs, including getting support from others when they are distressed.

Motivation

Motivation enables children to take an active and enthusiastic part in learning and it involves the ability to focus and work towards specific goals. Motivation is linked to skills of persistence, independence and personal organisation. These skills give children a much greater sense of control over the challenges they take on and how they set about them. Children who are motivated are more able to resist distraction, direct their attention, overcome frustration and bounce back after setbacks.

Empathy

This enables children to see something from another person's point of view, to anticipate their thoughts and feelings and to modify their own behaviour in the light of this. Empathy helps children to realise that they have the potential to make others feel better or worse. It also enables children to understand that other people experience the world in different ways and express themselves differently.

Social skills

Social skills enable children to relate to a range of other people and to take an active role in group activities. They come to understand what makes, breaks and sustains friendships, and what they need to do to co-operate and get on in a group. Being assertive, resolving conflicts and making wise choices are all part of developing social skills and learning for life.

HANDOUT 1.3

Achievement shield

Something I have achieved

Something I am proud of

Something I have taught my child to do

Something I would like to achieve

HANDOUT 1.4

Things that I like and that I am good at...

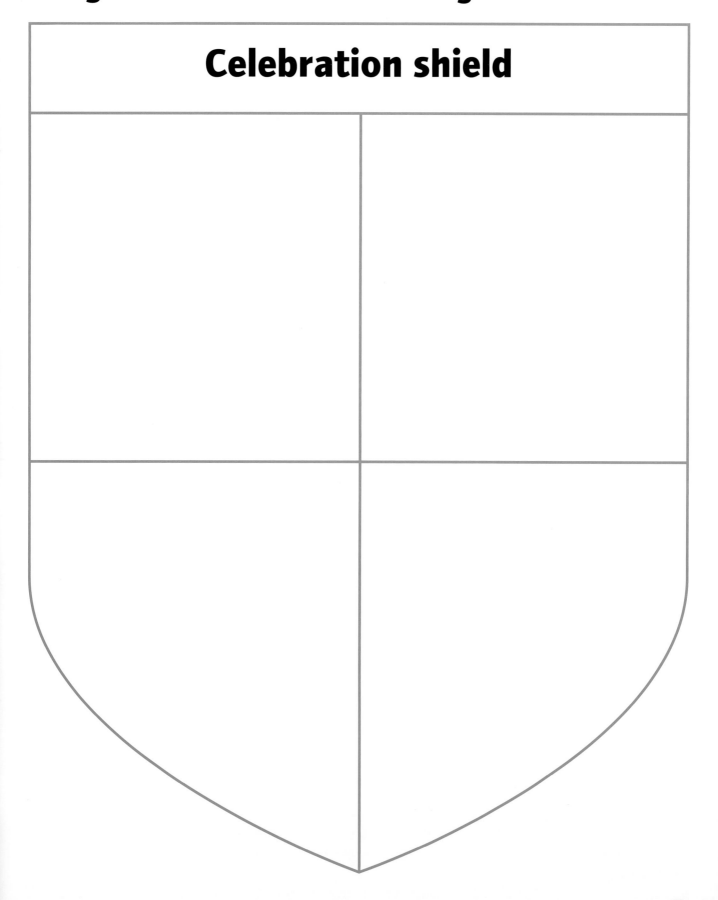

Celebration shield

Note: Evaluation forms for other sessions are available on the CD-ROM

Evaluation form

Name

For each question, please mark the line at the appropriate point to indicate your response

1) I enjoyed today's session

Not at all ⟵⟶ very much

2) The content of the session was interesting

Not at all ⟵⟶ very much

3) The group discussion was good

Not at all ⟵⟶ very much

4) The group exercises were helpful

Not at all ⟵⟶ very much

5) The input from the trainers was useful

Not at all ⟵⟶ very much

6) I felt able to contribute to the session and say what I wanted to

Not at all ⟵⟶ very much

7) One thing that I liked about today's session is:

8) One thing I would change about the session is:

Thank you!

SESSION 2:
What are the barriers to learning and what can we do about them?

TIMETABLE

Section	Timing	Materials
1. Starter	**10.00–10.15**	Handout 2.1 *Children learn what they live*
2. Feedback from home practice: Celebration shield Aims of the session	**10.15–10.40**	Carers' completed celebration shields Slide
3. The importance of education	**10.40–10.45**	Slides
4. Group quick-think: barriers to learning	**10.45–11.10**	Flip chart and slides Handout 2.2 *Looked after children and their education*
5. Pairs exercise: how does your child get on at school?	**11.10–11.35**	Handout 2.3 *Exercise: How does your child get on at school?* Flip chart
6. Discussion: learning something new	**11.35–11.45**	Flip chart
7. Pairs exercise: mirror writing	**11.45–12.15**	Handout 2.4 *Exercise: Mirror writing*
8. Break	**12.15–12.35**	Refreshments
9. Group exercise: exploring empathy	**12.35–1.05**	
10. Small group exercise: supporting learning – what matters most?	**1.05–1.35**	Flip chart sheets Handout 2.5 *Supporting effective learning: what matters most?*
11. Home practice: building on positives	**1.40–1.50**	Handout 2.6 *Home involvement in learning* Handout 2.7 *Supporting children with their learning*
12. Evaluation	**1.50–1.55**	Evaluation form
13. Closing round	**1.55–2.00**	Carers' achievement shields (from last session) Optional – chocolate/fruit to end the session

Welcome carers as they arrive.

RESOURCES

Name labels
Flip chart, pens
Laptop, CD-ROM with Powerpoint presentation, projector, screen
Refreshments
Optional chocolate or fruit

HANDOUTS

Please print these from the CD-ROM supplied and give each carer a copy of the handouts for today.

2.1 *Children learn what they live*
2.2 *Looked after children and their education*
2.3 *Exercise: How does your child get on at school?*
2.4 *Exercise: Mirror writing*
2.5 *Exercise: Supporting effective learning: what matters most?*
2.6 *Home involvement in learning*
2.7 *Supporting children with their learning*
Evaluation form

15 minutes

STARTER

Direct carers' attention to Handout 2.1, *Children learn what they live.* Ask for a volunteer to read this out. Then ask each carer to identify and share one lesson that they learnt from their childhood.

Start off the round by giving your own example, such as: 'I learnt very early on that, if I told the truth when I'd done something wrong, I would be understood.'

25 minutes

FEEDBACK FROM HOME PRACTICE

Celebration shield

Invite each carer in turn to show their child's shield and to describe how this activity went. Did anything surprise them? How easy or difficult did their child find it to think of positive things to say about themselves? How easy did the carer find it? How did the child respond to the activity as a whole?

Record the main points on the flip chart. Thank carers for bringing in their work and sharing their experiences.

If carers did not manage to carry out this exercise, you may want to find out what prevented them. Did they understand the task? Did it seem relevant to them?

Life for foster carers can be extremely stressful and there may be times when there is too much going on for them to focus on additional tasks. It is important that they are not made to feel guilty. The home practice tasks, however, do provide an opportunity for carers to get to know the children in their care a little better and to come back and reflect with the group on their children's needs.

Introduce the aims of today's session.

AIMS OF TODAY'S SESSION

- Explore the barriers to learning and success
- Get in touch with how it feels to learn something new
- Explore how carers can use empathy to support children's learning
- Identify the wide range of skills that carers can bring to support learning

5 minutes

THE IMPORTANCE OF EDUCATION

Explain to the group that education is important in determining the chances we have in later life.

THE IMPORTANCE OF EDUCATION

'The single most important indicator of children's life chances is educational attainment.' (DH and DfES, 2000)

However, for some children, educational success is elusive. As a group, looked after children perform significantly less well than their peers.

EDUCATIONAL OUTCOMES FOR LOOKED AFTER CHILDREN

Looked after children are:

- Ten times more likely to be excluded (SEU, 2003)
- Nine times less likely to leave care with 5+ GCSEs A*–C grades
- Nine times more likely to have a statement of special educational needs

25 minutes

GROUP QUICK-THINK

Barriers to learning

Ask carers to think about why some looked after children struggle with their learning so much more than their peers. What kinds of events and circumstances may create barriers to looked after children learning and getting the most out of school?

Write up carers' ideas on the flip chart.

Note for trainers: Some ideas might be: pre-care experiences, trauma and abuse, low self-esteem, lack of necessary skills, special needs not addressed, lack of constant adults to act as advocate, effects of numerous and unplanned moves of home and school, missed periods of schooling, lack of continuity in relationships, mistrust of adults due to previous experiences, bullying, poor planning and co-ordination on the part of the local authority, insufficient value placed on education, low expectations, insufficient support to catch up after disruption, exclusion, and so on.

To conclude your discussions on the barriers to learning, use the following two slides.

WHAT RESEARCH SAYS...

- pre-care experiences – separation, abuse and trauma
- broken schooling
- low expectations of looked after children
- low self-esteem
- lack of continuity of care-giver and of school

(Jackson and Martin, 1998)

Research suggests that there are a number of strands that contribute to the educational underachievement of looked after children.

In 2006, Barnardo's carried out a survey among a small sample of care leavers.

WHAT LOOKED AFTER CHILDREN SAY...

'Everyone...treats you like an idiot because you are in care.'

'Teachers assumed that because you were in care that you wouldn't make anything of yourself.'

'I had a behaviour problem and I was treated like I was incapable of achieving anything.'

(*Failed by the System*, Barnardo's, 2006)

As these quotes illustrate, many young people in care are confronted by negative assumptions and low expectations.

There is more information on Handout 2.2, *Looked after children and their education.*

25 minutes

PAIRS EXERCISE

How does your child get on at school?

Divide the group into pairs. Explain to the carers that you want them to think broadly about all aspects of their child's school experience – the academic, social and emotional.

Ask carers to spend five minutes each sharing and discussing:

- their child's areas of strength and difficulty at school
- how their child's past or current experiences as a looked after child may impact on their experience at school.

They can make notes on Handout 2.3, *How does your child get on at school?*

When each person has had an opportunity to do this, invite feedback to the whole group.

10 minutes

DISCUSSION

Learning something new

Explain to carers that sometimes we lose touch with how vulnerable children can feel when they are learning something new and unfamiliar. We may forget quite how anxiety-provoking it may be to go to school every day, fearing that we may not understand what is asked of us and worrying about what others will think of us.

Ask the group to think about some of the things that they have found hard to learn as adults. Examples might be:

- using a DVD player/new mobile phone
- learning to operate a computer
- completing a Sudoku puzzle
- learning to drive
- following a new recipe
- helping an older child with homework you are unfamiliar with

Ask carers to identify the feelings and thoughts that were stirred up.

Carers may report feeling "useless" or "humiliated". They may feel that others are impatient or patronising with them, or intolerant of their slowness.

30 minutes

PAIRS EXERCISE

Mirror writing

This exercise is designed to help the group to further explore how it feels to be a new learner.

Divide the group into pairs and give each pair a copy of the mirror writing sheet (see Handout 2.4) Explain that you want one person in the pair to try and read the passage. After a few minutes, ask the other people in the pairs to have a try.

Allow enough time for the carers to fully engage with this exercise. Many people may find this exercise difficult and challenging, although they will find that they do improve with time. Make sure both members of the pair have a go.

Trainers can listen out for the kinds of comments carers make to each other (*I'm useless at this; I can't do this; This is stupid*; etc).

When the exercise has finished, take feedback in the large group and ask carers to share their experiences. You may want to direct the discussion by asking some of the following questions:

- What was your reaction when you were first given the text?
- What were your feelings as you tried to read?
- Did you understand everything you were reading?
- Were you automatically able to read words you had seen on a previous line?
- What can you learn from this experience that you can use when listening to a child read?

This exercise can be a powerful one. Ask carers to call out words that describe their response to learning something new.

Note for trainers: Examples might be: frightening, frustrating, alienating, confusing, overwhelming, humiliating, anxiety-provoking, threatening, anger-inducing and so on. (Of course, some people may also find it satisfying to master this new skill and feel pleased with themselves when they get it right.)

20 minutes **BREAK**

30 minutes

GROUP EXERCISE

Exploring empathy

Explain to the group that learning is part of everyday life – something we all have to do. Some learning situations can, however, create anxiety and pressure for many children and we need to take care that we do not feed into this by responding to them with criticism, disappointment or anger. We want to take this opportunity to explore some of our own responses and to start by acknowledging some of the things that can go wrong.

Trainers are to act out the following short scenario in which a child is reading a school book to their carer.

Scenario

Child: (frustrated and tense) *I don't want to do this. It's too difficult. I can't understand it – it just doesn't make sense! Arghhh! I'm so stupid!*

Carer: (sternly) *Come on, now. Don't make a fuss. You're being silly. This is easy – you can do it.*

Ask the carers:

- What does the adult do?
- How is the child likely to feel and what may be the effect upon them?

Suggest to the group that when learning is difficult many of us feel quite sensitive and we do not respond well to correction or criticism. Most children benefit from a supportive response, one which understands and acknowledges both the situation and their feelings. This might be thought of as responding with "empathy".

Empathy is a complex term. Ask the group what they understand "empathy" to mean. Empathy may be described as the capacity to *recognise or understand another's state of mind or emotion.* It is often characterised as the ability to "put oneself in someone else's shoes".

GROUP EXERCISE

Empathy practice

When children are angry and frustrated, it is not necessarily easy to be supportive and to use empathy. Sometimes it is just too hard to acknowledge our children's difficult feelings. The following scenarios can be used to encourage the carers to think about how they might use empathy to support their children with difficult and upsetting learning situations. There are three scenarios. Using just one may be sufficient, but there are three available.

Explain to the carers that you want them to simply practise responding with empathy without having to reassure, explain or problem-solve. You will guide them with this.

One of the trainers will need to act out the following scenarios. You will need to use your acting skills! It is not just words that convey feelings, but facial expression and body language as well.

Explain to the group that in each situation you are going to play the part of a child. In this first scenario you are making a card for a relative.

SCENARIO 1

You have made a card and you are trying to draw something very carefully on it. You look dissatisfied with what you've done. You try and change it and then angrily scribble all over it.

Ask the carers to:

- put themselves in the child's shoes and share with the group what they think the child might feel, for example, disappointment, frustration and anger;
- imagine what might be going on in the child's mind – what are they thinking to themselves? *For example, 'I'm rubbish at drawing'.*
  'Nothing ever turns out the way I want it!'
- ask the carers to identify what they could say to the child that conveys that they are trying to understand how they feel.

Put carers' ideas on the flip chart.

Examples might be:

'You seem really frustrated – you wanted to get your picture just right.'

'You were working so carefully on that card and it didn't turn out the way you wanted. That is really tough for you.'

Carers will have their own particular way of conveying empathy. The important skill that we want to practise here is simply acknowledging the child's thoughts and feelings, without at this stage trying to solve or reassure.

SCENARIO 2

You are a child trying to do some sums and you cannot work them out. You count on your fingers, scribble something on your paper, look confused, try again – and then sigh, slump your shoulders, put your head in your hands and look downcast.

Ask the group to go through the same procedure:

- identify what the child might be feeling
- think about what might be going through their mind
- think about how to convey to the child that you are in touch with this

Examples might be:

'You look so fed up. I know it's not easy.'

'It can feel really discouraging when you are learning something new. You probably feel like you'll never work it out.'

SCENARIO 3

You are a child who comes out of the school gates, pulls off his jacket, throws it on the ground and shouts: 'Stupid school! Stupid teacher!'

Ask the group to follow the same procedure and share their ideas.

Examples might be:

'Something has really upset you.'

'You sound really angry. Tell me what happened.'

Ask carers to think about what they have learnt from the exercise and what they might do to put any ideas into practice.

Using empathy to get alongside your child is one very effective and important way that carers can support their children. We want to move on now to think of some other ways in which carers can help their children to get the most out of their education.

Making a positive difference

Explain to the group that research tells us that parents and carers can make an enormous difference to children's school experiences and to their educational attainment. There are a vast number of different ways in which carers support their children in school. At different times, carers take on the role of: teacher, confidante, personal assistant, taxi driver, playmate, social skills coach, mentor, counsellor, motivational coach and so on – and the group may well add to this list.

30 minutes

SMALL GROUP EXERCISE

Supporting learning – what matters most?

Divide carers into two groups. Give each group a sheet of flip chart paper and a pen and ask them to number from 1 to 10 down the left hand side. Then ask them to look at Handout 2.5, *Supporting effective learning – what matters most?* This sheet has a list of tasks which all represent ways in which a carer might support a child.

Each group should create a "top ten" list of the most important tasks for the foster carer, starting with the most important at the top. Carers may want to add some of their own ideas to the list.

- One group is to think about the priorities they would have to help improve their child's sense of belonging at school.
- The second group is to prioritise the skills they would use to try and improve their child's performance in literacy and numeracy.

Allow plenty of time for discussion in the small groups and then ask each group to feed back, explaining their choice of tasks. Give them Handouts 2.6, *Home involvement in learning* and 2.7, *Supporting children with their learning.*

10 minutes

HOME PRACTICE

Building on positives

Explain to the carers that, for this week's home practice, you want them to support their child with something that they are interested in. This could be something the child has learnt about at school and has expressed an interest in or it could be an outside interest – football, baking, singing, drawing, cycling, fashion, construction games, dinosaurs...anything at all.

Explain that you want the carers to spend some time with their child pursuing this interest. The child may suggest what they would like to do or the carer may need to take the lead. This might involve talking, watching a relevant television programme, reading a magazine, researching on the internet or going on a trip. The carer might make something with the child such as a scrap book or a picture, or write a story. What is important is that the carer shows interest and support and responds to the child's enthusiasm.

Ask carers what ideas they have and support and encourage them with any specific plans.

Ask carers to come back next week and describe what they have done with their child and bring in any work to share with the group.

5 minutes

EVALUATION

Ask carers to complete an evaluation for the session.

5 minutes

CLOSING ROUND

Using the carers' achievement shields as you did in the previous session, ask carers to share something that they have done to support a child with learning a practical, emotional or social skill.

Finish the session by acknowledging the hard work everybody has put in. If possible, give everybody a special treat such as a chocolate or piece of fruit.

HANDOUT 2.1

Children learn what they live

If a child lives with criticism, they learn to condemn.

If a child lives with hostility, they learn to fight.

If children live with fear, they learn to be apprehensive.

If children live with pity, they learn to feel sorry for themselves.

If a child lives with ridicule, they learn to be shy.

But do not despair...

If a child lives with tolerance, they learn to be patient.

If a child lives with encouragement, they learn confidence.

If a child lives with praise, they learn to appreciate.

If a child lives with fairness, they live with justice.

If a child lives with security, they live to have faith.

If a child lives with approval, they learn to like themselves.

If a child lives with acceptance and friendship...

they learn to find love in the world.

Dorothy Law Nolte (1972)

HANDOUT 2.2

Looked after children and their education

'The single most important indicator of children's life chances is educational attainment.'
(DH and DfES, 2000)

Good school experiences are a key factor in resilience. If things are going well at school, children are more likely to be happy and well adjusted and placements are less likely to break down. Being successful at school is not just about academic success – joining in activities, feeling safe and free from bullying, being part of the school community and feeling accepted for yourself are all important and empowering aspects of school life.

As a group, looked after children do much less well at school than their peers.

- They are ten times more likely to be excluded (Social Education Unit (SEU), 2005)
- 6% left care with 5+ GCSEs A*–C grades (compared with 56% overall) (Evangelou M and Sylva K, 2003)
- 59% are not in education, employment or training on their 19th birthday (compared with 13% in general population)
- 27% have a statement of special educational needs (compared to 3% in the general population)
- 1% go to university, compared with 43% of the general population

There are many reasons for these poor outcomes. They could be summarised as:

- pre-care experiences
- broken schooling
- low expectations
- low self-esteem
- lack of continuity of care-giver

(Jackson and Martin, 1998)

What looked after children say...

'Everyone...treats you like an idiot because you are in care.'
'Teachers assumed that because you were in care that you wouldn't make anything of yourself.'
'I had a behaviour problem and I was treated like I was incapable of achieving anything.'
(Barnardo's, 2006)

'Barnardo's' survey suggested that many young people feel that they are treated differently because they are in the care system. They are confronted by a range of negative assumptions about their abilities, their motivation and their behaviour.'
'Young people value highly carers who take a personal interest in their school life in a sensitive way, and who will come along and support them when they participate in school activities.'
(Ritchie, 2003)

'High educational achievement among care leavers is associated with placement stability and having a carer who values education.'
(Jackson and Martin, 1998)

HANDOUT 2.3

EXERCISE:
How does your child get on at school?

Think broadly about academic, social, emotional and other skills:

Strengths

Difficulties

What impact might their past or current experiences as a looked after child have on their progress at school?

Strengths

Difficulties

HANDOUT 2.4

EXERCISE: Mirror writing

SHE heard the news on the little transistor radio her granddaughter had sent her from the States. She who had lived so long she felt drained of all emotion, now experienced nothing but a confirmation of the news which had come floating down in scraps and whispers last year: her grandson was a thief, a murderer, a hired gunman, a rapist, a jailbird, a jail breaker, and now, at nineteen, a man with a price on his head.

From the time the first scraps of news had made their way from town, even as she expressed disbelief to keep up appearances, she knew that everything they said about him was the truth. She firmly believed that every evil deed, evil thought, of all the generations had finally been distilled into this one boy. Ever since the beginning when he had left home, she had coldly cast her mind back to every thing she knew about every single member of the family to discern if there was something hidden in her tribe that betokened this ending, and she could find nothing that warranted such a hard and final cruelty. They had faced deaths starvation hurricane earthquake cholera typhoid malaria tuberculosis fire dipthería and travel to dangerous and distant places in search of work. But beyond everything that they did, Ma Bell saw them as nothing more than victims struggling against the forces of a God who was sometimes deaf and blind.

Still, Ma Bell found the Lord a comforting presence. Since the last grandchild had left - the rapist, the thief, the hired gun, the murderer - Ma Bell had got into the habit of talking directly to the Lord. He was everywhere. She spent so much of her life in the consolation of his company that she could easily conduct dialogue with him for she knew his answers so well. And without having to let him know her whereabouts, she could continue her conversation with him anywhere in the house, in the yard, walking slowly and painfully down the lane to the Pentecostal Church of Christ the Redeemer. All her life, since she had first given birth at sixteen, sixty years ago, Ma Bell had spent her time addressing children and she saw nothing incongruous about addressing the Lord in the same manner for he failed her and tested her as surely as they did. Now she addressed him on the subject uppermost in her mind:

"Is wanting to better yuself a sin? Then if is sin, we have sinned. But nothing more than that. I know yu going pick on me first. But dont bother. If I did give short in my higglering days it was because I needed it, Lord. Pickney a yard needing shoes and books and clothes so they could learn to hold their head up high. And dont you see that it was right after all? Look how they turn out. Dont you please? Granted them forget me. You even. They dont write. Sometime I would starve if it was for them. Once in a blue moon a get a letter with a two, three dollar. But Lord, I ever get news yet that any of them in prison? That any of them thief? That any of them is murderer? Eh? You answer me that for you know even more than I hear. Never mind that I take their children and raise them till their mumma and puppa get establish in foreign and sometime when they done get establish they forget all we poor one still a scuffle down here. But dont you think a little cutting corner here and there is worth it? Talk truth now."

"Ma B, Ma B," a hurried and anxious voice called from the doorway "You hear the news?"

"Come in, Jacob. Dont excite up yuself so. Yu know is not good for the pressure."

"Ma B you did have yu radio on? Yu hear the news bout Jacko? Ma B, two thousand dollar reward."

Jacob was Ma Bell's seventy-year-old nephew but since he had never acquired her calm, she treated him just like a boy.

She now said patiently, "Yes Jacob. Jacko is now big wanted man. So what yu expect me to do?"

HANDOUT 2.5

Supporting effective learning: what matters most?

What do you think are the most valuable ways to support your child in their learning at school?

1 Talk with your child about their day at school

2 Be patient and keep calm

3 Talk about the things you found difficult when you were at school

4 Have fun – be creative

5 Set up an area where the child can read and work undisturbed

6 Encourage your child to express their ideas and views

7 Ensure your child has the right uniform and appropriate equipment

8 Talk regularly with the classroom teacher

9 Attend school events

10 Play alphabet and word games

11 Learn multiplication tables together

12 Encourage hobbies and interests

13 Voice positive expectations of your child

14 Show an interest in what your child has learnt at school

15 Acknowledge and praise small achievements

16 Encourage your child to bring friends home to play

17 Make sure your child gets to school on time

18 Read books with your child

19 Take the initiative to discuss problems that your child has with teachers

20 Sit with your child when they do their homework

21 Take your child to the library

22 Find out about the techniques the teacher uses, e.g. for long division

23 Let the child know that you value them for who they are

24 ....

25 ....

HANDOUT 2.6

Home involvement in learning

Carer (or parental) involvement in children's learning has a dynamic effect on progress. Many researchers believe that the home presents the most powerful teaching and learning situation. When care-givers show interest in their children's experiences and activities, children's motivation and self-esteem grows.

Carers impact on children's achievements through:

- **Good "parenting"** A positive and enthusiastic style of relating promotes self-esteem in the child and improves motivation and personal aspirations. Carers with a "can-do" mentality will be more able to instil an active and optimistic attitude in their children.
- **Talking with the child** about school experiences and activities. This seems to have an important and beneficial effect on behaviour and attainment, affecting feelings of self-worth and motivation and school-related skills.
- **The promotion of positive attitudes, values and aspirations** When carers communicate that they value their child's learning and education, this impacts on the child's perception of their school experience and work and bolsters their motivation.
- **Involvement with school** When carers talk to teachers and attend school functions, it helps children to feel that their carers have an interest and investment in their school experience. When care-givers and school share similar values and expectations about behaviour, attitudes and work habits, children tend to thrive. Good communication allows information to flow between school and home. It enables carers to keep children well-informed about school expectations and rules, as well as supporting the school to respond appropriately to children's changing needs and circumstances. Carers should be encouraged to be proactive in communicating with the school rather than waiting until problems develop.
- **Home structures that support learning** and provide support, incentives and discipline for the completion of homework.

HANDOUT 2.7

Supporting children with their learning

Things that can help:

- Showing interest in your child's learning
- Talking with your child about school experiences
- Support with early reading
- Making sure they get to school on time
- Working proactively to create positive communication channels with the school
- Checking whether there is homework to do and providing support and encouragement with this
- Praising and acknowledging small achievements
- Voicing positive expectations of your child and what they are capable of
- Peer support – friends who have done well who model school success and involvement
- Older role model or mentor
- Continuity and stability at home and school
- Attending school events and helping the child to access educational resources
- Support with out-of-school interests
- Taking swift action when things go wrong at school, e.g. bullying or difficulties with learning
- Giving support and advocating on behalf of your child

SESSION 3: How to work with schools and support children's education

TIMETABLE

Section	Timing	Materials
1. Starter: using my senses	**10.00–10.15**	Handout 3.1 *Using my senses* Prepared cards
2. Feedback on home practice: supporting your child's interests Aims of the session	**10.15–10.45**	Any work completed and brought in by the carers Slide
3. Learning styles Exercise: supporting your child's learning style	**10.45–11.00** **11.00–11.10**	Slides Handout 3.2 *Learning styles* Flip chart
4. Celebrating talents and abilities Game	**11.10–11.20** **11.20–11.25**	Slides
5. Discussion: supporting positive learning habits	**11.25–11.40**	Slide Flip chart
6. Quick-think: homework – associations – purpose – distractions	**11.40–12.00**	Slide Flip chart Handout 3.3 *Homework*
7. Break	**12.00–12.20**	Refreshments
8. Group exercise: creating positive learning routines	**12.20–12.40**	Flip chart sheets and pens Handout 3.4 *Fostering positive learning habits*
9. Introduction to supporting literacy Quick-think	**12.40–1.10**	Flip chart Slide Handout 3.5 *Pre-reading skills*
10. Activity: having fun with literacy	**1.10–1.40**	Glue, paper, scissors, glitter, play-dough, fabric, flyers, magazines to cut up, etc
11. Home practice	**1.40–1.50**	Creative/craft materials for carers to take home
12. Evaluation	**1.50–1.55**	Evaluation form
13. Closing round	**1.55–2.00**	Carers' achievement shields

Welcome carers as they arrive.

RESOURCES

Flip chart, pens
Laptop, CD-ROM with Powerpoint presentation, projector, screen
Post-it notes
"Sense cards" – cards which you have prepared to represent the five senses (see Handout 3.1)
Materials for exercise: glue, paper, stickers, sequins, glitter, scissors, magazines, flyers, play-dough, feathers, foam shapes/sheets, etc
Refreshments

HANDOUTS

Please print these from the CD-ROM supplied and give each carer a copy of the handouts for today.

3.1 *Using my senses*
3.2 *Learning styles*
3.3 *Homework*
3.4 *Fostering positive learning habits*
3.5 *Pre-reading skills*
Evaluation form

15 minutes

STARTER

Using my senses

(You will need a set of cards representing each of the five senses, which you will have prepared in advance. You can use the ones on Handout 3.1 – cut and mount on cards.)

Without looking at the pictures, choose a card. Now look at the card and describe something that you like about that particular sense. For example, the "smell" card might produce the association, 'I love the smell of newly baked bread!' Shuffle the cards and pass them on to the next person until everyone has had a go.

30 minutes

FEEDBACK ON HOME PRACTICE

Supporting your child's interests

Ask each carer in turn to report briefly on what they did and how the child responded. If they have brought any examples of what they did, make sure they have an opportunity to share these. It is important that you, as trainers, are encouraging and affirming to anyone who has been able to do something, however small.

Write up some of the main points on the flip chart.

Introduce the aims of today's session.

AIMS OF TODAY'S SESSION
- Exploring individual learning styles
- Identifying how foster carers can support learning routines
- Exploring pre-reading skills and having fun supporting literacy

15 minutes

LEARNING STYLES

Explain to the group that we do not all learn in the same kind of way and that we will start today's session by thinking about the individual differences in our approach to learning.

In order to learn, we depend on our senses to process information around us. Most people tend to rely on one of their senses more than the others and this determines their dominant learning style. There are three main learning styles.

LEARNING STYLES
- Visual learner: relies on seeing things in order to learn best
- Auditory learner: relies on hearing
- Kinaesthetic learner: likes to move around and try things out

Explain to the group that you are going to show three slides so that carers can work out what their learning style is. Read these out:

1) When you have to spell a word you are not sure about, do you:
a) try and see the word in your head?
b) try and sound it out?
c) write it down to see if it feels right?

2) After you have met someone for the first time, do you:
a) forget their name but remember their face?
b) forget their face but remember their name?
c) forget name and face but remember what you did/what happened?

3) When you are waiting somewhere, do you tend to:
a) look around – watch someone or something?
b) talk to yourself or someone else?
c) fidget, doodle or draw?

If carers answered mainly A, they are visual learners. If they answered mainly B, then they are auditory learners. If they answered C, they are kinaesthetic learners. Handout 3.2 explains these different learning styles.

Use the following slide to summarise:

KEY IDEAS
- We all learn in different ways
- Carers and their children need to understand how they learn best
- Carers can support children's preferred styles of learning

- Some teaching methods favour certain learning styles, and this can be challenging for those who prefer a different approach

10 minutes

EXERCISE

Supporting your child's learning style

Explain to the group that when children learn something new it is helpful for them to learn it in a way that is accessible and memorable. In the large group, ask carers:

1) How might they help a five-year-old with a preference for kinaesthetic learning with counting and basic adding and subtraction?

Note to trainers: Ideas might be:

- Use tangible objects for simple addition or subtraction – toy cars, bricks, sweets, pasta, etc
- Encourage the child to move around and to pick things up
- Encourage the child to practise counting whilst climbing up the stairs, skipping, jumping, etc

2) What are the different things carers might do to support a child learning their times tables if the child were: a) a visual learner; b) an auditory learner; and c) a kinaesthetic learner?

Note to trainers: Ideas might be:

- Visual learner: display posters with tables on, make drawings, encourage the child to write them out
- Auditory: use chanting, singing, listening to a tape/CD
- Kinaesthetic: encourage your child to move tangible objects, or to recite tables as they clap, dance, jump or skip – see what works!

10 minutes

CELEBRATING TALENTS AND ABILITIES

Explain to the group that valuing and celebrating abilities and achievements is important as it improves motivation and self-esteem. However, many children and adults do not think of themselves as particularly clever. This may be partly because we tend to think of intelligence in a very specific and narrow way. There is now increasing acceptance of the idea that there is a broad range of skills that are necessary in order to live life fully and successfully. These are sometimes referred to as "multiple intelligences".

Use the following slide to explore the different aspects of intelligence.

MULTIPLE INTELLIGENCES

If this needs clarification, explain that:

- Body smart refers to good motor co-ordination, as used in sport and dance
- Word smart is the ability to use language to express oneself, or to learn new languages
- Music smart means skills in performance, composition, and appreciation of music
- Art smart means appreciation of art, and skill with colours, patterns and shapes
- Think smart refers to problem-solving ability
- Number smart means mathematical and logical thinking
- Eye smart means being good at building, designing, using maps and solving visual puzzles
- Feelings smart refers to understanding your own needs and feelings
- People smart means understanding and getting on well with others
- Nature smart means being good at observing and understanding nature

Use the next slide to suggest that it is empowering to identify what we are good at.

IDENTIFYING WHAT WE ARE GOOD AT

Rather than asking, 'How **clever** am I?'

ask instead...

'HOW am I clever?'

This simple re-ordering of words puts the emphasis on identifying what we are good at, rather than trying to evaluate our general ability. This is a much more empowering way to think about ourselves. This is equally important when we are talking about our children.

5 minutes

GAME

Ask the group to stand in a circle and instruct them all to turn to the left so they are looking at the next person's back. Each person is to pick one of the skills from the 'How are you clever?' slide that applies to them. Go around the group, with each carer acknowledging one way in which they are smart. For example, you might say, 'I'm body smart – I have a talent for dancing'. After everyone has had a go, instruct each carer to pat the person in front of them on the back!

15 minutes

DISCUSSION

Supporting positive learning habits

Explain to the group that carers have an important role in helping their children to develop positive learning habits which enable them to focus and to organise themselves. These are important life skills that can be applied to homework, learning any new task or pursuing any interest.

Find out from carers:

- whether their children have to do any kind of homework for school
- whether they think the amount of homework their children are given is appropriate.

Note to trainers: You may need to accommodate discussion around homework and routines to the needs of your group and the children they care for. Some of the ideas for consideration may need adapting for children who have behavioural or learning difficulties. It is also worth exploring how young children who have little or no homework can be encouraged to engage in activities that develop thinking skills, concentration and persistence. They will benefit from, for example, drawing, doing puzzles, playing with construction toys or building models rather than just watching the television or playing computer games.

Explain that homework practice varies across schools but that government guidelines on homework suggest the following:

HOMEWORK

- Years 1 and 2: maximum of 1 hour a week on reading, spelling, literacy and numeracy
- Years 3 and 4 : maximum of 1.5 hours a week focused on literacy and numeracy, with occasional assignments in other subjects
- Years 5 and 6: maximum of 30 minutes a day with emphasis on literacy and numeracy but ranging widely over the curriculum

20 minutes

QUICK-THINK

Homework

Explain to the group that you are going to think about various aspects of homework together. You will be asking three questions for the group to address. The first one is:

i) What do you really think about homework?

Ask the group to give their associations to the word "homework". What is the first word or phrase that comes into their heads? They can draw on their memories of doing homework as a child and on their experience as an adult helping children with their homework.

Note to trainers: Responses might include: *boring; a chore; a challenge; a burden; routine; obligation; a necessary evil; absorbing; empowering;* and so on.

This exercise may tease out divergent beliefs about the value of homework within the group. Some carers may be staunch supporters while others may be sceptical about its value.

ii) What is the purpose of homework?

Ask carers to think about what skills homework can develop for their children and how these might be of benefit.

Write their ideas on the flip chart.

To summarise this, show the following slide:

BENEFITS OF HOMEWORK

- Homework enables the child to:
  - practise and consolidate specific skills
  - develop persistence, patience, concentration, independent learning routines and organisation skills
  - improve self-esteem, motivation and confidence
  - prepare for further study and work

When homework is appropriate to the child's individual learning needs, it has a number of different benefits. However, when homework is either too easy or too difficult, it can be damaging and de-motivating. If homework is not appropriate for the child's ability, carers should speak with the teacher as soon as they can to find a solution.

iii) What distracts children from their homework?

One of the great difficulties with homework is the problem of managing the many distractions that get in the way. Using the flip chart, ask carers to call out their experiences of this and make a list.

Note to trainers: Distractions may include: television, food, computer, other children, adults, toys, general noise and activity in the house, phone calls, visits by social worker and other professionals. Children may also lack the necessary skills or motivation to organise structured learning activities without adult support.

Conclude this discussion by making the point that most children need adult support to help them focus and settle on a task. Many will need supervision and ongoing praise and encouragement to keep them motivated. Handout 3.3, *Homework,* summarises these points.

20 minutes **BREAK**

20 minutes

GROUP EXERCISE

Creating positive learning routines

Divide carers into two groups and give them a sheet of flip chart paper. Ask them to share with each other their ideas for establishing positive learning routines for reading or doing homework. Suggest that they may want to think about:

- how to encourage children to settle down and concentrate
- how to manage distractions

Ask the groups to make a list of their top tips for fostering positive learning routines. This does not need to relate exclusively to homework. The ideas may apply to encouraging children to engage in independent reading, art, music or other hobbies and joint activities with the carer.

Ask both groups to feed back their ideas in the large group. If appropriate, you may supplement this with ideas from Handout 3.4, *Fostering positive learning habits.*

30 minutes

INTRODUCTION TO SUPPORTING LITERACY

Remind the group that they will be starting work on "paired reading" next week. Explain that learning to read is very significant and forms the basis of so much else that happens in school. There is overwhelming evidence about the important part that parents and carers play in developing children's literacy skills.

"Pre-reading skills" are the skills that most children acquire naturally in their pre-school years and which form the basis for later reading and learning skills. It is primarily through everyday, nurturing interactions with a care-giver that neural connections are formed in the brain which lay the foundations for later learning. Due to their early experience, some looked after children have missed out on some of these early stages of development.

Explain to the group that because babies spend a great deal of time sitting or lying down, they are reliant on those around them to provide stimulation.

Quick-think

Ask carers to think about the five senses – touch, sight, hearing, smell and taste. Ask them to suggest what kinds of activities and everyday interactions might facilitate babies' learning, growth and development. Write these up on the flip chart.

Supplement carers' ideas by using the following slide.

ACTIVITIES THAT FACILITATE BRAIN DEVELOPMENT IN BABIES

- Talking – in particular, a sing-song voice that uses pitch and rhythm
- Music, singing and chanting – aids memory, creativity and relaxation
- Gentle rocking and swaying movement – benefits balance and co-ordination
- Watching bubbles, feathers, mobiles – improves hand–eye co-ordination
- Looking at picture books with big, bold images
- Pointing and saying the names of things
- Praising baby enthusiastically when they respond to anything
- Letting baby feel and chew books and objects, where appropriate
- Saying the name of something and asking baby to point

Use the following slide to consider the kinds of activities that are beneficial for the development of literacy in pre-school children (two–four-year-olds).

ACTIVITIES THAT BENEFIT PRE-SCHOOLERS

- Matching games with shapes, patterns and letters
- Playing with rhymes – poems and nonsense rhymes
- Recognising letters – the way they look and sound

- Developing language skills – stories, conversation, poetry, etc
- Developing eye–hand co-ordination – drawing and scribbling
- Learning about concepts of print – how we look at books, follow print, turn pages and look at pictures, etc
- Using environmental print – reading letters and words in the world around us, such as signs, adverts and shop names
- Visiting the library

There is a substantial body of evidence to support the idea that children who are encouraged with these kinds of activities are likely to do better in their reading and other achievements later on in their school life (Evangelou and Sylva, 2003). Some of these activities, such as recognising letters, are more clearly "educational" in nature than others, but we should not underestimate the value of more basic human skills such as talking and listening. Encouraging the child to voice their opinions and to recount stories, listening to them attentively and engaging in appropriate conversation together all have a powerful effect on children's development and facilitate a variety of linguistic, social, cognitive and emotional skills.

Refer carers to Handout 3.5, *Pre-reading skills.*

30 minutes

ACTIVITY

Having fun with literacy

Ask carers to form into pairs or groups of three who care for a child of a similar chronological or developmental age. Each group is to create a simple game or activity which would enable their child to have fun exploring some aspect of literacy.

Make available a range of resources such as glue, crayons, play-dough, scissors, magazines, flyers, chalk, stickers, string, feathers, foam sheets, stencils, fabric, glitter, coloured paper and so on.

This activity should be fun, creative and engaging. Some carers may need you to give them some initial ideas to stimulate their own creativity.

Note to trainers: Carers with young children will need to make the game simple and stimulating, using visual, physical, tactile or other stimuli. Some ideas might be to:

- Cut some large letters from a foam sheet or fabric and make a name plate for their child's bedroom door
- Create a simple game where the child matches a picture of an object with the letter it begins with
- Make letters from play-dough to spell the child's name
- Create a clapping or chanting game with letters and words

Carers with older children could think about how they might have fun playing with words or sentences.

- Cut out words from magazines and flyers and use these to construct a nonsense sentence or rhyme
- Think of something that interests the child and create an activity around this: for example, a matching card game with pictures and names of footballers or animals

- Write a poem where the first letter of each line forms a name, motto or message when read vertically. For example a poem for "Megan" could be:
  Mornings are her best time
  Even when it's dark and cold
  Green and red are her favourite colours
  Always ready to play a game
  Night times she curls up in bed with her teddy

  Walk around the group and support carers with their ideas, giving suggestions where necessary. Some carers will be "in their element" and others will need help.

  At the end of the exercise, carers present their ideas and work to the group.

10 minutes

HOME PRACTICE

The task this week is for carers to use craft materials, magazines and flyers to have some fun with literacy. For younger children, this might simply involve finding together the letters to make up their name from old comics or magazines, etc, cutting these out and sticking them on some card to make a name plate for their bedroom door or a bookmark. The child could then decorate this with pictures, glitter or stickers. If you have letter cutters, you could make biscuits to form words or names. With older children you might cut out words or phrases from flyers and magazines and support your child to construct some simple poetry, funny sentences or even a very short story. Vary the complexity of the task to the child's ability. Be creative and have fun. Find out what other ideas carers have.

Ask carers to bring back their work next week to share with each other.

5 minutes

EVALUATION

Ask carers to complete the evaluation for the day.

5 minutes

CLOSING ROUND

Using their achievement shields, ask carers to share with the group a positive achievement in any area of their life.

HANDOUT 3.1

Using my senses

Cut these out and mount them on cards

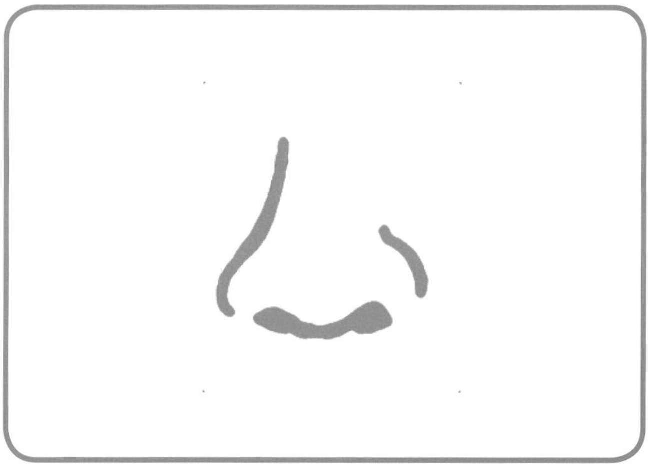

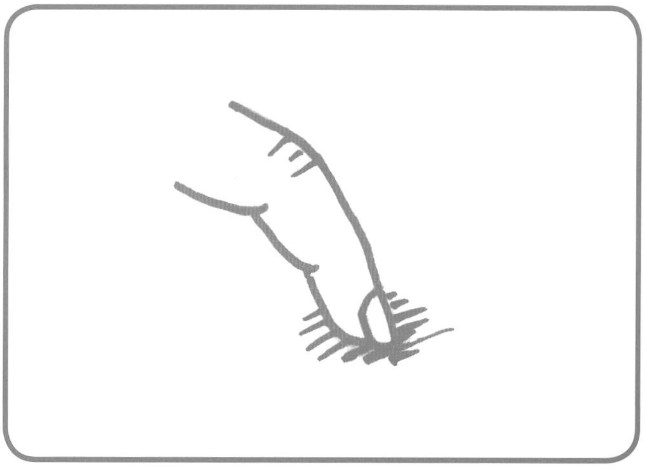

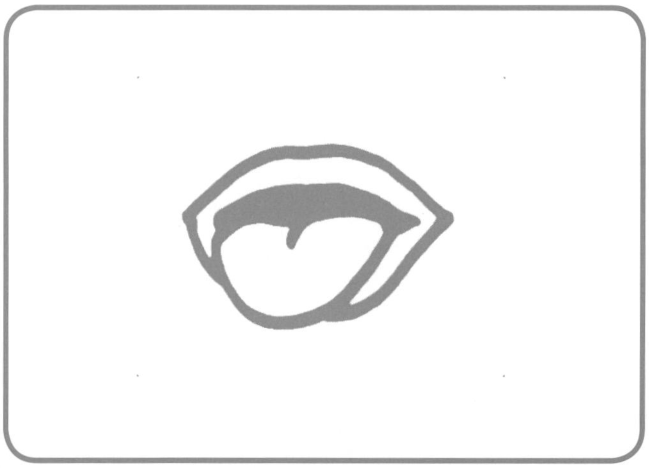

HANDOUT 3.2

Learning styles

There is no one right way to learn. Each person has their own preferred way of working and learning. What suits one person may not suit another.

Research on learning styles suggests that there are three basic kinds of learners.

The **visual learner** likes to see things and enjoys looking at instructions and getting information from books.

The **auditory learner** likes to learn through listening and so will like others to explain things to them rather than reading them themselves.

The **kinaesthetic learner** needs to learn by doing things and likes to move around and use their body. They remember things best by actually doing and experiencing them. Sitting still can be very difficult.

When children are learning something new or difficult, it may be helpful for them to learn it in a way that is most accessible and memorable for them. For example, a child who learns well through using movement may best learn to count by doing this walking up the stairs and counting each step as they go.

There are other factors which affect how well we learn or work:

- environmental factors – level of noise, light and temperature
- physical factors – preference for morning or evening, keeping still or moving around
- emotional factors – self-motivated or requiring encouragement
- social – preference for working alone or with others
- psychological – organised versus creative, impulsive or reflective, preference for routine or variety, interested in "big ideas" or in details

It is useful to bear these factors in mind when thinking about the conditions that will most support our children in their learning.

HANDOUT 3.3

Homework

Homework can be useful to consolidate skills learned at school, and it can also help children develop skills and habits which will support life-long learning. Current government guidelines on the appropriate amount of homework are:

- Years 1 and 2: maximum of 1 hour a week – reading, spelling, literacy and numeracy
- Years 3 and 4: maximum of 1.5 hours a week, focused on literacy and numeracy, with occasional assignments in other subjects
- Years 5 and 6: maximum of 30 minutes a day, with emphasis on literacy and numeracy but ranging widely over the curriculum

How can carers help with homework?

- Show interest – talk about homework
- Read letters from school that tell you what your child is working on in class
- Create a place where your child can read or work that is pleasant, light and warm and as free of distraction as possible
- Support your child but do not take over
- Make homework fun, where possible
- Be encouraging – not critical
- Give specific praise for effort and achievement
- Let your child know that you value education
- Keep in touch with your child's teacher

Setting up a regular routine

- Decide how much time your child will spend doing homework or reading each day
- Decide how much time your child can spend watching television and playing computer games
- Discuss with your child when, where and with whom they will do their homework. Write it down and post it up!
- Support your child in breaking down larger homework tasks into smaller, more manageable steps. Your child can tick these off as they complete them.

Children often need support to learn how to organise themselves. Create a checklist for any tasks that your child finds challenging. For instance, this could be getting ready to go to school, or coming home, or practising their spelling.

Checklist for coming home

- Put all my books and pencils in my bag
- Check for letters from school
- Get my coat and put it on
- Pick up my sports bag
- Leave school
- Walk straight home

HANDOUT 3.4

Fostering positive learning habits

- Set up a regular and predictable after-school routine – snack, homework/reading, television
- Decide when, where and with whom homework is to be done
- Use when...then instructions – '**When** you have done your reading, **then** you can play on the computer'
- Create a place where your child can read or work – as free of distraction as possible; keep it light and warm and pleasant
- Make homework fun, where possible
- Support your child with their homework but do not take over
- Give specific praise for effort and for achievements
- Show interest in your child's homework and talk about what they have learned today
- Model appropriate television and computer use
- Encourage reading time
- Enjoy time together in creative games and joint learning activities

HANDOUT 3.5

Pre-reading skills

These are the skills that most children acquire naturally in their early life and which form the basis for later reading and learning. It is the interaction between infant and care-giver that creates connections in the brain which are the foundation for intelligence.

Babies

Various campaigns encourage parents and carers to talk and read with their babies. Talking facilitates the development of language skills, and in the longer term aids listening, learning, reading, writing and socialising. As babies' mobility is limited, they are reliant on those around them to provide stimulation. Infants are responsive to sound, sight, movement, touch, smell and taste.

Activities which benefit babies

- Talking in a slow sing-song voice – letting the baby enjoy the rhythm and pitch of your voice
- Singing and chanting aids memory and creativity
- Music stimulates the brain and gains the baby's attention. It can also aid memory, improve co-ordination and facilitate relaxation
- Gentle rocking and swaying seem to benefit balance and co-ordination
- Watching bubbles or feathers moving in front of the baby's face helps with visual tracking and improves eye and hand co-ordination
- Looking at picture books with simple, large and bold pictures
- Pointing, saying the names of things
- Praising the baby when he/she responds to anything
- Saying the name of something and asking baby to point
- Letting the baby feel and chew books, where appropriate

Pre-school children

Activities which have been shown to benefit pre-school children

These are linked with improved reading scores and general school achievement.

- Matching games – with shapes, patterns and letters
- Playing with rhymes – poems and nonsense rhymes
- Recognising letters – the look and the sound of them
- Learning that print (in the English language) goes from left to right
- Developing language skills through talking, listening, hearing poetry and stories, joining in conversations, etc
- Developing eye–hand co-ordination through drawing and scribbling
- Learning about "concepts of print": how we look at books, turn pages, follow print, look at pictures and so on
- Using environmental print to help your child learn about reading and about the world around them. This is the print that you see everywhere – shop names, road signs, adverts that come through your door and so on
- Visiting your local library together

SESSION 4:
Paired reading: supporting children's literacy

TIMETABLE

Section	Timing	Materials
1. Starter: "My favourite story"	**10.00–10.15**	
2. Feedback from home practice: having fun with literacy Aim of the session	**10.15–10.45**	Slide
3. Exercise: carers' experiences of learning to read	**10.45–11.10**	Slide Flip chart
4. Introduction to paired reading	**11.10–11.15**	Slides Handout 4.1 *Paired reading: what are the advantages?* Handout 4.2 *What to read, when to read and where* Handout 4.3 *Paired reading: how to do it*
5. Paired reading Part 1	**11.15–11.45**	DVD *Paired reading* Part 1 Slides
6. Paired reading Part 2	**11.45–12.05**	DVD *Paired reading* Part 2 Slides
7. Break	**12.05–12.25**	Refreshments
8. Paired reading Part 3	**12.25–12.45**	DVD *Paired reading* Part 3 Slides Handout 4.4 *Praise for reading* Handout 4.5 *Paired reading record card*
9. Paired reading Part 4: paired reading for children with minimal reading skills	**12.45–1.05**	DVD *Paired reading* Part 4 Slides
10. Paired reading practice Quick think: praise for reading	**1.05–1.30** **1.30–1.40**	Suitable reading material Flip chart
11. Home practice	**1.40–1.50**	
12. Evaluation	**1.50–1.55**	Evaluation form
13. Closing round	**1.55–2.00**	

Welcome carers as they arrive.

RESOURCES

Flip chart, pens
Paired reading DVD
Laptop, CD-ROM with Powerpoint presentation, projector, screen
Appropriate reading material ranging from very simple stories with a few words to more complex text for older readers
Refreshments

HANDOUTS

Please print these from the CD-ROM supplied and give each carer a copy of the handouts for today.

4.1 *Paired reading: what are the advantages?*
4.2 *What to read, when to read and where*
4.3 *Paired reading: how to do it*
4.4 *Praise for reading*
4.5 *Paired reading record card*
Evaluation form

15 minutes

STARTER

'My favourite story when I was little, and why I liked it'

Ask each carer to share with the group one of their favourite stories or books from their childhood and say why they liked it.

30 minutes

FEEDBACK FROM HOME PRACTICE

Having fun with literacy

Ask carers to describe what they did with their child and to show any examples of what they made or did together. Give enthusiastic praise for any work that was done.

Introduce the aim of today's session

AIM OF TODAY'S SESSION

- Introducing the "paired reading" literacy scheme

25 minutes

EXERCISE

Carers' experiences of learning to read

Ask the group to form pairs. Ask each individual in the pair to share with their partner their own experience of learning to read. The following slide might help to provide some focus for this.

LEARNING TO READ

- Where did you learn to read – at school, at home?
- With whom did you learn?
- What are your memories of this experience?
- How easy or difficult was learning to read?
- Did you read with adults in the home?
- Did you have your own books?
- Did you enjoy reading?

Ask the group for some feedback. Recognise that this exercise may stir up painful memories. Some carers may have struggled with learning to read and may have felt negatively about themselves or about those who were meant to be helping them. There may also be some carers for whom books featured very little. Some may have only hazy memories of learning to read.

5 minutes

INTRODUCTION TO PAIRED READING

Use the following slide to introduce paired reading.

PAIRED READING

- is a well established reading scheme
- has been developed by Professor Keith Topping at Dundee University
- has been extensively evaluated and proved to be effective
- can be used with children with a wide range of abilities
- builds on and develops the relationship between the child and the carer
- is relatively non-technical
- will not conflict with other reading schemes the child is using at school

Many children will be using phonics as part of their literacy approach at school. Paired reading takes a different approach and does not involve the sounding out of words. Reassure carers that the paired reading will not interfere with alternative literacy strategies used in school. Encourage carers to look at Handout 4.1, *Paired reading: what are the advantages?* If carers are at all concerned, they can inform the class teacher that they will be using paired reading with their child over the course of the next few weeks.

LIKE ANYTHING NEW, PAIRED READING REQUIRES THAT WE UNDERSTAND:

- what it is
- how it works
- what skills it requires
- the need for practice, time and commitment

Explain to the group that they will be watching a DVD where foster carers use paired reading with children. The DVD has four sections and you will pause after each for clarification and discussion. Refer carers to Handout 4.2, *What to read, when to read and where* and Handout 4.3, *Paired reading: how to do it.*

30 minutes

PAIRED READING PART 1

Play Part 1 of the DVD.

When this has finished playing, give carers an opportunity for questions and then use the following slides to clarify and discuss any further issues.

WHAT TO READ

- books – fact or fiction – newspapers, comics, magazines, information printed off the internet
- material selected by the child and which is of interest to them
- material from school or from home
- visit your local library and let your child select something from the wide range of material on offer

Carers will need to talk to their child to try to find out what they might like to read. The child will be much more motivated if they read something that interests and excites them.

LEVEL OF DIFFICULTY

- Books should not be so easy that the child can read them successfully alone
- They should not be so hard that the child can read very few of the words
- It is important that the adult who is supporting the child can read the material fairly easily

Carers should choose material that is not only of interest to the child but that presents some degree of challenge. There needs to be the right balance of familiar and unfamiliar words.

THE FIVE-FINGER TEST

- Ask the child to spread their five fingers over a page in the book or other material they have chosen and touch any five words
- Can the child read all the words their fingers touch?
- Try another four pages (20 more words)
- The adult should be able to read all of these words successfully
- The child should be able to read fewer

This test is designed to help carers judge what might be an appropriate book to use for paired reading. If the child can read about three-quarters of the words, then the material is probably at the right level. Carers need to understand this simple test so they can identify the most appropriate reading material for their child.

WHEN AND WHERE

- Read with your child at least three times a week – daily if possible
- Aim to read for about 15 to 20 minutes
- Find somewhere that is quiet and comfortable
- Sit comfortably side by side so that you can both see the book

As well as identifying suitable reading material, carers need to find the right time and place to read with their child.

TALKING ABOUT THE TEXT

- Talk with your child about the material you are reading before you start, during the reading and at the end
- Pause when appropriate to discuss the words and the pictures and to make sure that your child has a good understanding of what they are reading
- Relate the subject matter to the child's life if it is helpful

Talking with the child about the book is important. If appropriate, carers can start the paired reading time by talking with the child about the cover and title of a book and discussing what they think the book will be about. This helps to provide a meaningful context for reading.

THE BENEFITS OF TALKING

- It makes reading together more relaxed, relevant and fun
- It deepens the child's understanding of what is being read
- It extends vocabulary
- It builds the relationship between the carer and the child

Discussion should be relaxed and gentle and not leave the child feeling that they are being quizzed or interrogated!

Carers need to understand that the aim of asking questions about the meaning of a word or passage is not to test the child or catch them out, but instead to create opportunities to explore the text and learn.

20 minutes

PAIRED READING PART 2

Play part 2 of the DVD and give carers an opportunity to comment and ask questions. Follow this up with the slides and further discussion.

READING TOGETHER

- Begin paired reading by reading together with the child
- Match your pace, tone and phrasing to that of the child
- Try to gently shape your child's reading by modelling phrasing and expression
- Point to words only if you really have to (don't make a habit of this)

To start, the carer and the child need to read **together**. The carer will need to pay careful attention to the pace and tone of the child's reading. The carer should use appropriate expression, phrasing and intonation. If the child is reading too quickly, the carer may try to gently slow them down by reading more slowly themselves. The carer is trying to influence the child but not to dominate the reading or distract the child. It is not helpful to point to the words on the page, so the carer should try to avoid doing this.

MISTAKES WHEN READING TOGETHER

- If your child gets a word wrong when you are reading together, pause and wait for them to put it right (up to four seconds)
- If they don't put it right, you say the word correctly, then ask your child to repeat the word, then carry on reading **together**

- Remember, it's OK to say that you don't know a word. Don't guess if you don't know, but try to find out

It can take time and practice to get used to pausing for four seconds and waiting for the child to correct the word without jumping in. The carer should not sound out the word or give prompts to the child, but simply allow them space to work it out if they can. After the pause, the carer should just say the correct word.

20 minutes **BREAK**

20 minutes

PAIRED READING PART 3

Play part 3 of the DVD. Allow for comments and questions and then use the following slides.

READING ALONE

- Agree on a signal for your child to give when they want to read alone (e.g. a tap, a knock or a nudge)
- At the signal, praise the child and stop reading together
- The child continues to read the passage alone

When the child feels confident or reaches a passage in the book which they feel able to read alone, they can give a signal to the carer to let them know that they want to stop reading together and to continue reading on their own. The carer should always praise them for doing this.

MISTAKES WHEN READING ALONE

- If the child makes a mistake when reading alone, pause for four seconds to give them the opportunity to correct it themselves. If this happens, praise them and then they can continue reading alone
- If they cannot put it right in this time, you say the word, ask the child to repeat it, and then go back to reading together
- Later, the child may signal again, and begin to read alone again

When the child reads alone, it is important that they read accurately and carefully. If they make a mistake, miss a word or mispronounce a word, the carer must make sure they say the word correctly. Once they have done this, carer and child carry on reading together, although the child can signal to go solo again as soon as they wish. So there is a cycle of reading together, reading alone, reading together, reading alone, and so on.

PRAISE

- Praise often, using different words
- Praise and smile – sound like you mean it!
- Praise your child for reading hard words or long sections
- Praise your child for correcting their own mistakes
- Praise your child for their effort and persistence

Praise is very important in paired reading. Some of the praise carers give will have to be done swiftly as the child is reading. When carers pause to discuss the text they can give some more specific and descriptive praise, letting the child know exactly what they have done well. For example, 'You read for a long time without making any mistakes!' or 'You worked out some really difficult words, well done!' Refer to Handout 4.4, *Praise for reading*.

The paired reading record card

- Use Handout 4.5, *Paired reading record card*, to reflect on how the reading session has gone.
- Use it to provide positive feedback to the child for anything they have done well.

Carers will have a copy of Handout 4.5, *Paired reading record card*, in their handouts for today. Encourage carers to use the record card this week and in all following weeks to reflect on how both they and their child are getting on. If carers complete the record card at the end of their time reading with the child, they can also use it as an opportunity to give positive feedback and specific praise to the child.

20 minutes

PAIRED READING PART 4

Paired reading for children with minimal reading skills

There may be carers in the group whose children have little or no reading skills. Part 4 of the DVD shows one way to adapt the paired reading approach by making a book which is tailored to the individual child's interests and learning needs.

Play Part 4 of the DVD and take questions and comments.

Use the following slides to summarise this section.

MAKING A BOOK

- Use photographs, drawings or pictures that the child finds interesting
- Involve your child in making the book – work on one page at a time
- Use simple words and short sentences (two or three words)
- Use words that the child hears or uses in everyday speech, familiar names and simple concepts

---

The book might be about the child themselves, or about something they are interested in. Start by making the first page together. Have the child choose a picture and paste it on the page. Invite the child to comment on the picture. Write down their words underneath the picture. You can add to the story as and when the child is ready – go at their pace. For children with very limited literacy, use high frequency words – names of family members, or basic but significant words and concepts from everyday use.

USING THE BOOK

- The carer reads the words to the child
- The child then reads with the carer (repeat this stage as often as needed)
- In time, the child may read the words by themselves
- The carer can add to the book day by day or week by week

Summing up and further questions

Provide an opportunity for carers to ask questions and discuss any issues that they may have about the paired reading approach. Remind them that nobody ever learns a new skill without practice and it always takes time.

25 minutes

PAIRED READING PRACTICE

Using the selection of children's books, comics and magazines, ask the carers to choose something that is close to their child's reading level or something they feel comfortable reading in the training situation.

Ask the carers to form pairs. You may need to give some thought to which carers you put together, especially if there are carers in the group with reading difficulties or little confidence.

One of the pair needs to take the role of adult and the other, the role of child. Explain to the carers that the person taking on the role of the child should try and read as a young child would – faltering slightly, stumbling over some words, struggling with others.

Allow plenty of time to practise. As they practise, spend some time listening to each of the pairs. Give specific praise where carers are trying hard or using the approach accurately and appropriately. Guide and encourage where necessary. Some carers may:

- tend to read too quickly, and not "follow" the "child"
- find it very hard to pause to allow the "child" to correct themselves
- try to prompt or encourage the "child" to sound out the word
- forget to praise
- forget to stop to discuss the text

Encourage carers to follow the guidelines and to use the approach as accurately as possible.

After 10 minutes or so, ask the carers to swap roles so that everyone has an opportunity to try out both roles.

Reconvene the group and take feedback on how it felt to be in the adult and child roles.

- What was easy and what was difficult?
- Was this a pleasant experience or did it feel strange or uncomfortable?

Paired reading is likely to be a rather unfamiliar way of reading for many carers. Reassure the group that with practice they will be able to do it well and they will find it rewarding!

10 minutes

QUICK-THINK

Praise for reading

Ask carers to think about what aspects of their child's reading they might praise and what they might say. Write down the carers' ideas on the flip chart.

Handout 4.5, *Praise for reading*, reminds us that we can praise the child for many different aspects of their reading. We can praise them for effort, even if they make many mistakes. Praise can also be given for accuracy, for reading with style or expression, for making improvements, for co-operating or for concentrating.

10 minutes

HOME PRACTICE

Encourage carers to practise paired reading at least three times during the coming week, and more often if they can. Ask them to use the paired reading record cards to track how they get on and to bring this back with them next week to feedback to the group.

5 minutes

EVALUATION

Ask carers to complete the evaluation for the day.

5 minutes

CLOSING ROUND

Ask carers to call out one idea from the session that they found particularly interesting or helpful.

HANDOUT 4.1

Paired reading: what are the advantages?

- Children are encouraged to pursue their own interests when it comes to choosing what to read. They have more enthusiasm for reading about their own favourite things, and so try harder. Paired reading gives them as much support as they need to read whatever book they choose.
- Children are more in control of what's going on: instead of having reading imposed on them, they make decisions themselves (e.g. about choice of books, going on longer than 10 minutes and going on to reading alone).
- There is no failure – it is impossible not to get a word right within five seconds or so.
- Paired reading is very flexible – the child decides how much support is necessary according to their current level of interest, mood, degree of tiredness, amount of confidence, difficulty of the books, and so on.
- The child gets lots of praise – it's much nicer to be told when you're doing well, instead of being pulled up when you go wrong.
- There's lots of emphasis on understanding – getting the meaning out of the words – and that's what reading is all about. It's no use being able to read the words out loud mechanically without following the meaning.
- Paired reading gives continuity – it eliminates stopping and starting to "break up" hard words. Doing that often leaves children having forgotten the beginning of the sentence by the time they get to the end. With paired reading it is easier for children to make sensible guesses at new words, based on the meaning of the surrounding words.
- While reading together with an adult, a child can learn (by example) to read with expression and the right pacing, e.g. by copying how the adult pauses at punctuation or emphasises certain words.
- Children are given a perfect example of how to pronounce difficult words, instead of being left to work it out themselves and then perhaps thinking their own half-right efforts are actually 100% correct.
- When doing paired reading, children get a bit of their own peaceful one-to-one attention from their carers, which they might not otherwise have had. There is some evidence that just giving children more attention can actually improve their reading.
- Paired reading increases the amount of sheer practice at reading children get. Because children are supported through books, they get through them faster. The number of books read in a week goes up, the number of words children look at in a week goes up and more words stick in the child's memory.
- Paired reading gives carers a clear, straightforward and enjoyable way of helping their children – so no one gets confused, worried or bad-tempered about reading.

...so children have more interest, confidence and understanding.

HANDOUT 4.2

What to read, when to read and where

What to read

- Books, magazines and newspapers
- From school, home or library
- Child should choose the book
- Too hard for child to read alone
- Not too hard for the helper
- If the book isn't right – choose another one!

When to read

- Little and often
- 10–15 minutes a day
- 5 days a week, if possible
- For 6–10 weeks initially

Try to ensure that other helpers in the house read with your child in the same way.

Where to read

- The quietest place you can find
- Somewhere comfortable
- Side by side
- Where you can both see the book easily

HANDOUT 4.3

Paired reading: how to do it

Talk!

- Show an interest in the book
- Talk about pictures
- Discuss the meaning of difficult or unusual words/phrases
- Talk about story or content
- Listen and give thinking time
- Talk to make sure that your child understands

Praise!

- Praise very often
- Praise for reading hard words
- Praise for reading a whole sentence or paragraph correctly
- Praise for putting words right without help
- Use a variety of praise words
- Show pleasure – smile, hug...

Correcting!

When your child says something wrong:

- You say it correctly
- Child must say it correctly

Then carry on reading together (before your child forgets the rest of the sentence!)

Pause before correction

- Give 4–5 seconds before correcting
- Let the child self-correct if they can
- Give rushing readers 2–3 seconds:
- And point back to the word

Reading together

- Both you and child read words exactly together
- Match your speed to your child
- Your child must read every word

Pointing

- Point only if needed (on hard books or small print)
- It is best if the child points, rather than you

Reading alone

- Agree a signal for you to go quiet (tap, nudge, etc)
- At child's signal, you go quiet and...
- Child reads out loud alone

Correction when reading alone

- If your child does not self-correct in 4–5 seconds:
- You correct, and...
- Begin reading together again
- Child signals when they are ready to read alone again

Enjoy paired reading with your child!

HANDOUT 4.4

Praise for reading

For effort

- Absorbed
- Dedicated
- Determined
- Persistent
- Resolute
- Tenacious
- Tireless
- Wanting to succeed
- Putting lots of effort in
- Tackling hard words
- Keeping at it
- Working hard

For accuracy

- Accurate
- Careful
- Getting the knack
- Few mistakes
- Taking more care
- Thorough
- Skilful
- Perfect
- Precise
- 100%
- Competent
- Flawless
- Impeccable

For reading style

- Accomplished
- Careful
- Clear
- Confident
- Dynamic
- Expressive
- Fluent
- Has a go at hard words
- Steady pace
- Masterful
- Sensitive
- Taking initiative

For getting better

- Best yet
- Blossoming
- Coming on a bunch/a treat
- Forging ahead
- Full marks
- Has never read better
- Improving all the time
- Making great strides
- Making headway
- Progressing in leaps and bounds
- Breakthrough

HANDOUT 4.5

Paired reading record card

Book read	Time spent	Observations
Monday		
Tuesday		
Wednesday		
Thursday		
Friday		
Saturday		
Sunday		

SESSION 5: Paired reading practice with the carer and their child

Please remember that this session is not like the others. It is less about "learning" from a course and more about observing actual practice and coaching where necessary.

Aims

- To observe the carer and child doing paired reading
- To provide accurate feedback to the carer on their paired reading skills
- To ensure that carers have understood and can apply the principles of paired reading
- To offer encouragement and praise

Practice is an important part of developing and acquiring any new skill. Carers and children should be reading together using the paired reading approach at least three times a week. Carers will need to work on their skills to ensure that they are providing the best possible support to their children. Although paired reading is a relatively non-technical approach, it still needs practice and guidance in order to do it well.

Giving and getting feedback is an important part of practice. This session provides an opportunity for you to observe carers reading with their children and to provide encouragement, guidance and feedback. You can make sure carers understand the fundamental skills of paired reading and are putting them into practice.

Organisation

This practice session needs to follow on from Session 4, ideally within a week or two. As this session involves the children, you will need to think about whether you want to arrange this in a half-term break, on a Saturday, or in individual after-school sessions. As there are a variety of ways of organising this, you will need to think about it and plan well in advance depending on local circumstances. Options include:

- You can visit the carer and child at home to hear them read. If you do this, you will need to be confident that you can have undisturbed, good-quality time with the carer and child. You will need to negotiate with the carer in advance to ensure that this is possible.
- You can choose a suitable venue and invite each carer and their child to attend for their own individual paired reading appointment. This could be after school, during a half-term break or at a weekend. This can provide quite an intimate and unhurried context for practising and you can provide refreshments and small rewards for attending.
- Another option is to organise a special meeting of the group. You will need a venue that is large and flexible enough to accommodate everyone. You will need space to hear carers and children reading, as well as adequate room for alternative activities and refreshments for those who are waiting to read.

Holding this meeting in a library can work well – the librarian can introduce children and carers to their services and to the books and other materials. Many libraries also have access to local children's writers, storytellers or other resources. The event could also include visits by significant people from your work organisation or local community. The meeting then also acts as a celebration of the work of foster carers and the achievements of the children.

These arrangements require careful planning and co-ordination and you will need additional staff to ensure adequate support and supervision.

Listening to carers and children read

How you introduce the paired reading practice will depend on the setting and arrangements you have made. However, you will want to put children at ease and help everyone feel as comfortable as possible. Thank the children for coming and explain that the meeting today is to see how their carer is getting on with paired reading. It is important that the children do not feel scrutinised – tell them they are helping out by providing an opportunity for their carer to practise their skill.

The carer and child are then to do paired reading. Trainers will need to think about all the components of the paired reading approach, from the selection of appropriate reading material and the way that the carer and child sit together, to the variety of techniques involved in the reading itself.

You need to combine observing and listening, giving feedback and offering support and praise. You need to make sure the carer and the child have adequate space to practise, while getting sufficient support to improve their skills. Give both the child and the carer plenty of specific praise for the things they do well. Do not be afraid to intervene to model skills or to encourage the carers to practise specific skills, such as giving praise or discussing the text. If carers are not correcting children's mistakes, explain the procedure slowly and clearly so that both the carer and the child understand.

Your observation will provide you with a good picture of the carers' paired reading skills as well as insight into any particular difficulties they might be having in reading with their child. Encourage carers to work on any aspects of the reading skills that need further improvement.

Seeing carers putting their skills into practice is a rewarding experience, and it is an opportunity to provide them and their children with praise and affirmation.

The end of the session should be marked by a small acknowledgment for both the child and carer. One agency taking part in the paired reading scheme made personalised, laminated bookmarks for each of the children. Another bought a selection of comics and magazines for children to choose from and to take home.

SESSION 6: Supporting learning through the use of praise

TIMETABLE

Section	Timing	Materials
1. Starter	**10.00–10.10**	
2. Feedback on paired reading Aims of the session	**10.10–10.40**	Flip chart Slide
3. Role play and discussion: paired reading	**10.40–11.00**	Child's reading book for practice
4. Small groups exercise: Quiz: understanding the education system	**11.00–11.30**	Paper for small groups and flip chart Handout 6.1 *The education system: some basic information*
5. Small groups exercise: supporting looked after children with their education: who does what?	**11.30–12.00**	Slide Flip chart Downloaded publication *Who does what?*
6. Break	**12.00–12.20**	Refreshments
7. Quick-think: the experience of praise	**12.20–12.35**	Flip chart Slides
8. How to praise: the basics Quick-think: non-verbal aspects of praise	**12.35–12.50**	Slides Flip chart
9. Group discussion: targeting praise	**12.50–1.10**	Slides Flip chart
10. Pairs exercise: practice in giving praise	**1.10–1.40**	Handout 6.2 *Praise*
11. Home practice	**1.40–1.50**	Paired reading record card Handout 6.3 *Praise cards* Handout 6.4 *Home practice: giving praise*
12. Evaluation	**1.50–1.55**	Evaluation form
13. Closing round	**1.55–2.00**	

Welcome carers as they arrive.

RESOURCES
Flip chart, pens
Laptop, CD-ROM with Powerpoint presentation, projector, screen
Reading material for paired reading practice
Refreshments

HANDOUTS
Please print handouts from the CD-ROM supplied and give each carer a copy of the handouts for today.

6.1 *The education system: some basic information*
Who does what? (download from http://publications.teachernet.gov.uk/default.aspx?PageFunction=productdetails&PageMode=publications&ProductId=LACWDWSD&
6.2 *Praise*
6.3 *Praise cards*
6.4 *Home practice: giving praise*
Evaluation form

10 minutes

STARTER

Ask each carer to share one thing that strikes them as different when comparing their child's school and the school that they attended as a child.

30 minutes

FEEDBACK ON PAIRED READING

As this is the first opportunity carers will have to talk together about their experience of paired reading, make sure that each carer has enough time to describe how things have gone.

Ask carers to describe to the group in turn their experience of paired reading so far. They might use their paired reading record sheets to help with this. Carers should describe:

- what went well
- what was difficult
- how often they managed to read with their child
- how they found a suitable time and a comfortable space to read
- how they found suitable reading materials
- how their child responded

If carers struggled with finding suitable reading material, remind them that they can use newspapers, comics, internet resources and so on.

Introduce the aims of today's session.

AIMS OF TODAY'S SESSION
- Refine paired reading skills
- Develop our understanding of the education system and the carer's role within it
- Learn how to praise effectively
- Reflect on how we can use praise to encourage learning

20 minutes

ROLE PLAY AND DISCUSSION

Paired reading

One of the trainers should do a role play of a paired reading session, with their co-worker or one of the carers playing the child. The objective is not to perfectly demonstrate paired reading but to illustrate some of the problems that may be encountered so that the group has a chance to identify and discuss how problems could be solved. The person who is playing the part of the child should struggle with some of their reading.

Ask the carers to observe the role play and identify what the adult does well and how they could improve their paired reading skills.

When the feedback and discussion have finished, ask for two volunteers from the group to undertake another paired reading role play. Encourage further feedback and discussion, ensuring that it is accurate, balanced and constructive. Thank the two carers for taking part.

In both role plays, remember to take feedback from the "child" so that the group can reflect on the experience of paired reading for the child.

Note for trainers: This practice exercise provides an opportunity to reinforce the principles of paired reading. Be prepared to identify and discuss any of the techniques that prove to be difficult or are misunderstood. Common issues for discussion may include using praise effectively, talking about the text and managing mistakes.

30 minutes

SMALL GROUPS EXERCISE

Quiz: Understanding the education system

Supporting children's education through working closely with school staff is an important part of the foster carer role. However, the education system is continually evolving and not everyone is familiar with educational structures and jargon. This quiz is designed to share information and common knowledge and to stimulate discussion. (This information is correct at time of publication (June 2010), but please be aware that some of these terms and procedures may change over time.)

Ask carers to break into groups of three or four. Ask them to discuss together what they understand each of the following terms to mean, and to make some notes about this.

QUIZ: UNDERSTANDING THE EDUCATION SYSTEM
What do the following terms refer to?

- National Curriculum/Curriculum for Excellence
- Designated Teacher/Senior Manager
- PEP: Personal Education Plan
- Special Educational Needs/Additional Support Needs
- SATs: Standard Assessment Tests (England only)

When the small groups have finished, review the answers, comparing them to the definitions set out below. (Information is also available in Handout 6.1, *The education system: some basic information.*)

National Curriculum/ Curriculum for Excellence

The National Curriculum has to be followed by all state schools in England, Wales and Northern Ireland. It tells schools what children must study and what they should know at certain ages. Children are tested at various stages to keep a check on standards.

In Scotland, a Curriculum for Excellence is being implemented in academic year 2010/11. It will create a seamless curriculum from age three to 18, and will offer pupils greater choice and opportunity.

The Designated Teacher/ Senior Manager (in Scotland)

This person has overall responsibility in the school for children in care. Their role includes: liaison with children's services and particularly social workers; working with carers and parents; and promoting supportive and inclusive policies for looked after children.

PEP (Personal Education Plan)

Every child in care in England and Wales must have a Personal Education Plan which sets out the child's educational needs, how these are to be met and the expected outcomes. The PEP should be agreed within 20 days of a child coming into care and be reviewed at least every six months (either at or close to the child's statutory review).

Children with special educational needs (SEN) or additional support needs (ASN)

Children who have special educational needs are entitled to extra help and support in school. The local authority makes a statutory assessment of the child's educational needs and, if it decides that the child needs extra help, they would write a Statement of Special Educational Needs, which will describe the child's needs and the help required to meet them (in England, Wales and Northern Ireland). A Special Educational Needs Co-ordinator (SENCO) ensures that children with special educational needs receive the right level of help and support – there is a SENCO in every state school. In Scotland, the term used is additional support needs.

SATs (Standard Assessment Tests) (England only)

At the end of each Key Stage – in Year 2 and Year 6 – children are assessed for their attainment against nationally set standards in English and mathematics, and in Year 6 only, science.

Keep the discussion relatively simple where possible and draw carers' attention to Handout 6.1, *The education system: some basic information.*

30 minutes

SMALL GROUPS EXERCISE

Supporting looked after children with their education: who does what?

This is an exercise to explore the respective roles of foster carer, social worker and teacher, who all share some responsibility for a child's education. Many of these responsibilities overlap. Show the following slide.

SUPPORTING CHILDREN WITH THEIR EDUCATION

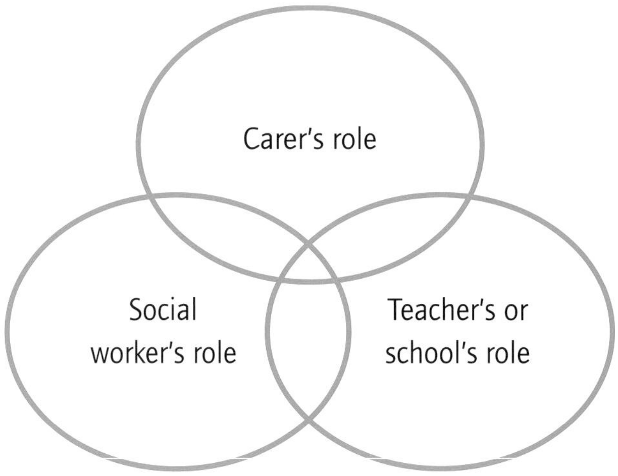

Divide the group into three small groups. Each group is allocated one of the above roles: social worker, foster carer, teacher/school. Ask the groups to make a list of up to 10 tasks that would support the child with their learning and education that fall within the remit of their role.

When the groups have completed their list, they should feed this back to the large group. This can be recorded on the flip chart.

Encourage questions and discussion and pay particular attention to overlapping roles or to any confusion of role and responsibility. Find out from the group where in their experience things work out well or go wrong, using examples where appropriate.

Note for trainers: Tasks may include:

- reading
- talking about school
- creating a sense of belonging at school
- attending parents' evening
- talking with teachers
- checking and giving support with homework
- looking out for signs that something might be wrong
- reading and responding to the child's school report
- talking with the school about bullying
- attending school events
- out-of-school hours learning

Provide the group with the downloaded handout *Who does what?*. This provides a checklist of responsibilities for social workers and foster carers in relation to the education of looked after children.

20 minutes **BREAK**

15 minutes

QUICK-THINK

The experience of praise

Explain to the group that in the coming weeks there will be a focus on the development of children's social and emotional skills and self-esteem in relation to learning. In this session, we begin by exploring one of the essential building blocks of self-esteem: praise.

Many adults feel that they get very little praise for what they do. But it is as important to adults as it is to children.

Ask the group to spend a few minutes identifying an experience where they were praised for something they had done. What was this praise for? What form did the praise take? How were they left feeling from this experience? Make some notes from the feedback on the flip chart.

Possible answers

Praise can help us to feel: proud, happy, confident, appreciated, valued, more content and relaxed.

It can also arouse uncomfortable feelings, like: embarrassment, suspicion, anger and unworthiness.

Acknowledge that praise can evoke uncomfortable feelings for some people. This may be particularly true for children who have developed a negative picture of themselves resulting from abuse and neglect. Use the following slide to explore this idea.

PRAISE WHEN CHILDREN HAVE BEEN ABUSED AND NEGLECTED

- Some children do not respond positively to praise
- They do their best to resist it
- They will need praise that is specific, frequent and low-key

You could use the metaphor of a dried sponge to describe the experience of giving praise to a child who rejects it. Drips of water may bounce off the hard exterior of a dry sponge. However, over time the drips will eventually soften the sponge and they will be absorbed. In a similar fashion, gentle, specific and persistent praise will help the resistant child to eventually absorb positive messages.

15 minutes

HOW TO PRAISE

The basics

Show the following slide to explore some of the benefits of using praise.

EFFECTIVE PRAISE CAN CHANGE MOOD, ATTITUDE AND BEHAVIOUR

It can help a child to feel:

- noticed and affirmed
- cared for and valued
- good about him or herself
- motivated to behave differently

However, not all attempts at giving praise are as helpful as others, so it is important to learn how we can give praise in the most effective way.

Ask the group what ideas they have for giving effective praise. What do they say to communicate their praise and affirmation? Discuss their ideas and use the following slides to underline some of the important aspects of praise.

EFFECTIVE PRAISE

- Provides positive feedback to the child about what he or she is doing well
- Is descriptive and specific

Explain to the group that the terms we use in everyday life, like "good girl" or "well done", do not communicate to the child clearly enough in a way that they can understand what it is that they have done well. In order to praise effectively, we need to be specific and to describe the behaviour that we like. Use the following slide to exemplify this.

EXAMPLES OF SPECIFIC AND DESCRIPTIVE PRAISE

'I saw you helping Carla find her shoes. That was kind, thank you.'

'You have written that letter beautifully and clearly. Well done!'

'You kept really calm when Jaydon teased you. I'm impressed. Good boy!'

Explain to the group that we can use praise to describe and affirm very different types of behaviour, and that children's behaviour is most likely to improve when we use this kind of specific praise consistently and frequently.

QUICK-THINK

The non-verbal aspects of praise

Praise is not just about what we say – it is also about how we say it and what we do. Ask the carers to describe the non-verbal aspects of giving praise. Write their ideas on the flip chart.

Sum up this exercise by using the following slide.

NON-VERBAL ASPECTS OF PRAISE:

Be:	**Use:**
warm	touch
enthusiastic and expressive	smiles
sincere	eye contact
	gestures – "high-five"

20 minutes

GROUP DISCUSSION

Targeting praise

In using praise to support and encourage children's learning and education, we need to think specifically about those behaviours we want to encourage. One way of doing this is to use targeted praise. Use the following slide to explain this.

TARGETING PRAISE

This involves:

- identifying the behaviour or skill that the child needs to learn
- looking out for a sign of that behaviour – however small
- giving both verbal and non-verbal and specific praise for the behaviour

The trick is to notice small signs and improvements and affirm these using praise. Show how this might work by using the following example.

TARGETED PRAISE WITH A TIMID CHILD

Q: *What behaviours might you want to encourage?*	**A:** Any bolder or more decisive behaviour
Q: *What naturally occurring behaviour might you be able to praise?*	**A:** The child stating an opinion or preference
Q: *What could you say to praise the child?*	**A:** 'You want spaghetti for tea? I love it when you tell me exactly what you want! Thank you!'

Using the following slide, ask the group to think through how they might give targeted praise to a child who is overactive.

TARGETED PRAISE WITH AN OVERACTIVE CHILD

Q: *What behaviours might you want to encourage?*	**A:** Being quiet, calm or focused
Q: *What naturally occurring behaviour might you be able to praise?*	**A:** You might notice your child waiting patiently, sitting quietly or playing co-operatively
Q: *What could you say to praise the child?*	**A:** 'Well done. You waited so patiently and quietly for your turn. I'm proud of you.'

Ask carers to think about a particular child. They should then identify one behaviour or skill that they think will help the child to get on better at school or become a more competent learner. Encourage them to think broadly about a range of practical and social behaviours as well as more academic ones.

Ask each carer to name one behaviour. Write these on the flip chart.

Examples could include:

- sitting still
- playing calmly with other children
- listening to instructions
- learning their alphabet
- holding a pencil
- learning their times tables

30 minutes

PAIRS EXERCISE

Practice in giving praise

Ask the group to break into pairs and explain to their partner the behaviour that they would like the child to develop or learn. Each pair is to think about how that behaviour might occur spontaneously in some small way. Each carer, in turn, should practise with their partner how they would give praise, using positive body language and enthusiastic, descriptive and specific feedback. Carers may feel slightly awkward practising praise with another adult, but rehearsing skills in training will improve the chances of success when they use the skills at home with the child.

Trainers should move around the pairs, giving clear and specific praise to the carers and providing guidance and support, where needed.

Afterwards, ask the group to give feedback. How did the group find this exercise? What was easy? What was more difficult? Do they anticipate any difficulties in using praise with their child this week?

Praising effort and achievement

Explain to the group that, when any of us are trying to learn something new, we need to pay attention to both the effort we put in as well as what we actually achieve. In order to remain positive and motivated, we all need to be praised for our efforts, even when we make mistakes or find that progress is not as quick as we would have liked.

So, for example, a child who is having difficulty with a homework assignment needs praise and affirmation for the effort they make, not just for completing the assignment or for the grade they get. The effort needs to be praised as well as the achievement. Trying hard and not giving up are invaluable life skills.

Handout 6.2, *Praise,* provides a brief summary of the content of this session.

10 minutes

HOME PRACTICE

- Encourage carers to continue paired reading with the child, reinforcing the importance of doing it at least three times a week. Encourage carers to complete a paired reading record card after each paired reading session.
- Carers should also practise using praise with the child, trying where they can to target specific behaviours using descriptive praise. Give the carers a selection of praise cards – some examples are available on Handout 6.3 which you can cut up. Carers will need to fill these in, using simple and age-appropriate language, and use them for rewarding both effort and achievement. The praise cards can be given directly to the children, and read to them where necessary, or left as a surprise on the child's pillow or in their lunch box, for example. Carers know the children in their care better than anyone – encourage them to think about how the child might react to finding or being given a praise card and adjust what they do accordingly.
- Draw carers' attention to Handout 6.4, *Home practice: giving praise*, on which they can record the praise they have given and any observations about the child's response.

5 minutes

EVALUATION

Ask carers to complete the evaluation for today's session.

5 minutes

CLOSING ROUND

Addressing each member of the group in turn, ask each carer to praise the person sitting next to them, using the ideas about praising that have been explored in the session.

HANDOUT 6.1

The education system: some basic information

This information is correct at time of publication (June 2010), but please be aware that some of these terms and procedures may change over time.

National Curriculum and educational levels

England, Wales and Northern Ireland

The National Curriculum has to be followed by all state schools in England, Wales and Northern Ireland. It tells schools what children must study and what they should know at certain ages. Children are tested at various stages to keep a check on standards.

Children's learning is planned and assessed through six areas:

1. Personal, social and emotional development
2. Communication, language and literacy
3. Mathematical development
4. Knowledge and understanding of the world
5. Physical development
6. Creative development

The foundation stage covers education for children aged from three to the end of reception year. Four key stages follow:

- Key Stage 1: for children in years 1 and 2 (aged 5–7);
- Key Stage 2: for children in years 3 to 6 (aged 7–11);
- Key Stage 3: for those in years 7 to 9 (aged 11–14); and
- Key Stage 4: for those in years 10 to 11, which is when most children take GCSEs or other national qualifications.

By the end of Key Stage 1, the teacher's assessment of progress would take account of the child's performance levels in English and mathematics. At the end of Key Stage 2, the child will take national tests in English, mathematics and science.

Scotland

In Scotland, a Curriculum for Excellence is being implemented in academic year 2010/11. It will create a seamless curriculum from age three to 18, and will offer pupils greater choice and opportunity. Curriculum levels are divided into:

- Early – the preschool years and P1 (P = Primary);
- the First level – to the end of P4;
- the Second level – to the end of P7; and
- the Third and Fourth levels, with the latter broadly equating to Scottish Credit and Qualifications framework level 4.

Children with special educational needs (SEN) or additional support needs (ASN)

Children who have special educational needs are entitled to extra help and support in school. In Scotland, the term used is additional support needs. In Wales, The Looked After Children Education Co-ordinator fulfills this role. The local authority makes a statutory assessment of the child's educational needs and, if it decides that the child needs extra help, they would write a Statement of Special Educational Needs, which will describe the child's needs and the help required to meet them (in England, Wales and Northern Ireland). A Special Educational Needs Co-ordinator (SENCO) ensures that children with special educational needs receive the right level of help and support – there is a SENCO in every state school.

Personal Education Plan (PEP)

Every child and young person in care (in England and Wales) should have a PEP which sets out academic achievement; identifies developmental and educational needs; and sets out short- and long-term targets and plans. The PEP should be part of the child's Care Plan. It also forms part of a pupil's curricular record, which the governing body has a duty to keep in respect of each registered pupil.

- The child's social worker is responsible for initiating the PEP but it is to be completed in partnership with the designated teacher, family, carers, child and other relevant parties.
- The Personal Education Plan should be agreed as soon as possible and within at least 20 days of a child entering care or joining a new school.

- The Personal Education Plan should be reviewed concurrently with the Care Plan and at least every six months. Carers should have copies of PEPs.

Co-ordinated Support Plan (CSP)

In Scotland, a Co-ordinated Support Plan is prepared for children with additional support needs. It outlines their additional needs; their educational objectives; and the support they will need to help them fulfil these. The CSP is a legal document, which means that the local authority must make sure that the child receives the support listed in the CSP.

The Designated Teacher/ Senior Manager

The Designated Teacher (in England) has overall responsibility for children and young people who are in care and it is their role to support them in their school life. They are to:

- Liaise with Children's Services and the other agencies that are involved.
- Promote inclusive policies and robust pastoral systems that promote a whole school ethos that is supportive to looked after children.
- Keep links with parents or carers and ensure that PEPs are up-to-date and home-school agreements are kept.
- Promote a climate of high expectations for attainment and behaviour for looked after children by raising knowledge and awareness.
- Maintain and share relevant information about children in a sensitive way so as to promote positive relationships and provide a foundation for a positive school experience for all concerned.
- Act as a resource for staff and pupils.

In Scotland, this role is performed by the Designated Senior Manager who is responsible for looked after children.

Individual Education Plan (IEP) or Individualised Educational Plan (in Scotland)

An IEP is an education plan or programme which is prepared for certain children and young people with additional support needs by their school. The plan should include short-term targets and actions for an individual child, the teaching strategies to be used, the help to be put in place, and how the school will decide if the help has been successful.

Pastoral Support Programme

A short practical intervention (in England) to provide support when a child is at risk of permanent exclusion. It is initiated by the school, but should be agreed with parents/carers and involve the local authority and other agencies, such as children's services.

Pupil Referral Unit (PRU)

In England, a PRU is an educational establishment for children who have been excluded from school or who are at risk of exclusion, or who cannot attend school for other reasons such as ill health, pregnancy or school phobia. In Scotland, similar provisions exist in the form of specialist units or schools, but are not called Pupil Referral Units.

Transition

Transition is change from one education stage to another. In schools, it usually refers to children moving from primary to secondary school. Children will cope better if they are prepared for such major changes, and nearly all schools now take great care to give parents/ carers information about these transitions.

Homework

Within home-school agreements, the government suggests that schools spell out homework policy so that parents/carers can establish approximately what each child should be doing at home on a weekly basis. Some schools use homework planners or diaries to record homework, and close contact with staff at the school can usually establish what is happening.

Inclusion

Inclusion means the right to be educated in a mainstream school alongside other children. The Centre for Studies on Inclusive Education defines it as 'disabled and non-disabled young people learning together – enabling pupils to participate in the life and work of mainstream institutions to the best of their abilities, whatever their needs'. The aim is for all schools to become inclusive schools, and welcome all pupils and develop values which promote pupils' educational, social and cultural development.

Exclusion

A child can be excluded on a permanent or fixed-term basis by the head teacher if staff at the school feel that they can no longer cope with the problems a child is causing. The school has to be able to show that great efforts have been made to change the behaviour of the pupil but that these failed, or that allowing the child to remain in school would harm the welfare or education of other pupils.

Common abbreviations

BSP	Behavioural Support Plan
CSP	Co-ordinated Support Plan
EBD	Emotional and behavioural difficulties
G&T	Gifted and talented
IEP	Individual Educational Plan/ Individualised Educational Plan
KS	Key stage
LSA/ TA	Learning Support Assistant/ Teaching Assistant
MLD	Mild learning difficulties
Ofsted	Office for Standards in Education
PSP	Pastoral Support Plan
PEP	Personal Education Plan
PRU	Pupil Referral Unit
PTA	Parent Teacher Association
SATs	Standard Assessment Tests
SEN	Special educational needs
SLD	Severe learning difficulties

HANDOUT 6.2

Praise

Praise is a powerful and effective way of communicating.

Most children are extremely responsive to adults when they notice their appropriate behaviour and comment positively and clearly about this. Praise affirms and encourages the child and makes it more likely that positive behaviours will occur again.

Praise can feel uncomfortable

Many adults and children are not entirely used to being praised and so they may feel awkward, embarrassed or mistrustful when it happens. Some looked after children may be particularly resistant to praise. They are likely to be the children who have been on the receiving end of overwhelming criticism, disapproval and disappointment and they may have learned to respond suspiciously or even defensively to praise. If carers continue to affirm these children and provide them with specific, frequent and low-key praise, they will eventually start to feel more positively about themselves.

How to praise

Praise is an accepting and affirming communication and it is best when it is done with personal warmth, enthusiasm and sincerity. The way we use our voice, our facial expression and our body can all add to the impact of our praise, but we need to gauge this to the style and needs of the child.

- Be warm
- Be appropriately enthusiastic
- Make eye contact
- Use touch and gesture
- Smile

Effective praise

What we say is also really important. It may be useful to think of praise as positive feedback: it provides the child with information about the behaviour that you like and value. So when you notice your child behaving well, rather than simply saying 'well done' or 'good girl', describe the behaviour that you see. Keep your praise frequent, specific and meaningful. This will be far more effective.

- 'I saw you playing really calmly with your friends. That was lovely. Well done!'
- 'You sat still all the way through that film. That was brilliant!'

What behaviour do you praise?

You can select any appropriate behaviour for praising. It may be helpful to think about the kinds of skills and qualities that your child needs to develop to become a more confident and effective learner. For some children, "listening to instructions" or "sitting still" might be the most vital skills for them to develop, whereas other children might need to work on learning their alphabet or their times tables. There is a whole range of academic, behavioural and social skills that we can encourage and praise.

Examples of behaviours to praise:

- sitting still
- co-operating
- listening attentively
- taking turns
- being polite
- keeping quiet
- saying sorry
- keeping hands to themselves
- following instructions
- being polite
- concentrating
- being patient
- accepting criticism
- keeping calm
- asking for help
- thinking before acting
- keeping trying
- trying new tasks
- creative writing
- skilful drawing
- knowing how to spell
- tuneful singer
- holding pen nicely
- good handwriting
- expressive reader
- knowing times tables
- speaking clearly
- knowing alphabet
- compromising
- accepting responsibility

Praise for effort!

When we praise effort, we help to build the child's motivation, and it is the act of keeping on trying that will ultimately bring results. Praising effort is more important than becoming fixated on performance or achievement. Children who are reluctant to take risks or who are frustrated by their level of ability will need frequent praise for their efforts in order to help them keep going. They will easily feel overwhelmed by failure and so you will need to break down tasks into small components and provide praise for each small step.

Using praise to enhance self-esteem

Self-esteem is linked to what others say about us and what we have come to believe about ourselves. Carers can use praise in a deliberate way to help children become more aware of their positive attributes and skills and thereby enhance their image of themselves.

Some ideas for enhancing self-esteem:

- Targeting praise: Think about the skills that your child needs to develop to become a more competent and effective learner – and then go out of your way to notice and praise any small sign of those behaviours. For example, you might encourage a timid child for stating a bold opinion; congratulate an overactive child for waiting their turn patiently; and praise the oppositional child when they do what they are asked immediately. When you provide specific praise, you will find that your child is more likely to repeat the behaviour.
- Linking behaviour to particular attributes: This can help to boost your child's view of themselves:

'Bianca, I saw you lend your pencils to Betty when she couldn't find hers. That's what I call "thoughtful".'

'Tariq, I saw you hold your tongue when Matt snatched your book. That takes self-control. Good on you.'

This kind of praise lets the child know that you value their positive actions and it can help them to recognise and attribute positive personal qualities to themselves.

- Building the connections between actions and consequences: Children can be helped to create positive links between their actions and desirable consequences. For example, you might say:

  'You worked hard on that piece of work. I think you should feel proud of yourself.'

  'Now that you have done your homework I think you can relax. How can you reward yourself for your effort?'

  This will help children to own their achievements and feel proud of themselves.

Praising ourselves

Some people may feel uncomfortable about voicing their own achievements or skills. Self-praise, however, is an important life skill and it can help us to value who we are and what we do, and enable us to maintain a positive and optimistic attitude. Self-praise is different from boasting, which involves making ourselves feel superior at the expense of others. Self-praise can be important for our motivation and well-being, and it also models the importance of recognising personal effort and achievement for the child.

Don't forget to notice and acknowledge your own hard work and achievements to yourself and others!

HANDOUT 6.3

Super!

presented to

because

Well done!

You've worked so hard at

For

You were amazing!

HANDOUT 6.3

To

....

we are so **proud** *of you*

because

....

....

To

....

Congratulations!

You have made an
AMAZING IMPROVEMENT in

....

....

Wow!

You really know how to

....

....

HANDOUT 6.4

Home practice: Giving praise

Praise given: when, where and how	Observations: what happened?

SESSION 7: Supporting self-esteem

TIMETABLE

Section	Timing	Materials
1. Starter: 'How's the weather with you?'	**10.00–10.10**	Slide
2. Feedback: paired reading Aims of the praise session	**10.10–10.45**	Slide
3. Group exercise: creating a climate in which children can flourish	**10.45–11.05**	Flip chart with sun and cloud illustrations Prepared post-it notes Handout 7.1 *Exploring self-esteem*
4. Group exercise: the origins of self-esteem	**11.05–11.20**	Rope and two signs: "brilliant" and "terrible" Flip chart and pens
5. Quick-think: self-esteem	**11.20–11.40**	Slides Flip chart
6. Input and discussion: the effects of self-esteem on learning	**11.40–11.50**	Slides
7. Input and discussion: the cycle of low self-esteem	**11.50–12.00**	Slide Handout 7.2 *The cycle of low self-esteem*
8. Break	**12.00–12.20**	Refreshments
9. Input: how I am and how I would like to be	**12.20–12.30**	Slides Handout 7.3 *Self-esteem*
10. Small groups exercise: supporting self-esteem	**12.30–1.00**	Slide Paper for group ideas Flip chart for feedback Handout 7.4 *Encouraging self-esteem*
11. Story-telling	**1.00–1.15**	Slides Flip chart
12. Group quick-think: good story-telling techniques	**1.15–1.20**	Flip chart
13. Group exercise: reading a story	**1.20–1.40**	Book to read in the group (for example, *Ruby and the Rubbish Bin*)
14. Home practice	**1.40–1.50**	Handouts *Paired reading record card,* Handout 7.5 *You're special*
15. Evaluation	**1.50–1.55**	Evaluation form
16. Closing round	**1.55–2.00**	Handout 7.6 *Building your own self-esteem* Optional treats to end the session

Welcome carers as they arrive.

RESOURCES

Flip chart, pens
Laptop, CD-ROM with Powerpoint presentation, projector, screen
Rope and signs for exercise
Prepared post-it notes for exercise
Book for group storytelling, for instance, *Ruby and the Rubbish Bin* (Margot Sutherland, Speechmark 2003)
Optional sweets/fruit or other treats for closing round

HANDOUTS

Please print handouts from CD-ROM supplied and give each carer a copy of the handouts for today.

7.1 *Exploring self-esteem: Creating a climate in which children can flourish*
7.2 *The cycle of low self-esteem*
7.3 *Self-esteem*
7.4 *Encouraging self-esteem*
7.5 *You're special*
7.6 *Building your own self-esteem*
Paired reading record card
Evaluation form

10 minutes

STARTER

'How's the weather with you?'

This exercise uses the weather as a metaphor to describe how group members have felt during the week. Show the slide of weather symbols and ask carers to describe their week using the symbols for weather as a starting point. You might start this activity by saying something like, 'I had a pretty mixed week – cloudy with sunny intervals. My son was sick and needed a lot of looking after, but I had a lovely day on Sunday when an old friend visited.'

HOW'S THE WEATHER WITH YOU?

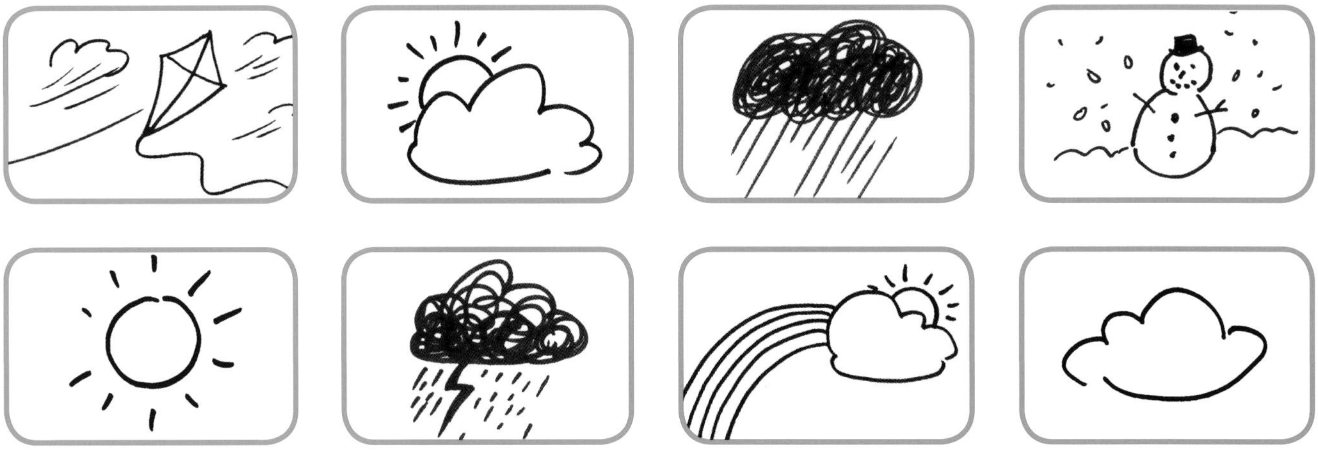

35 minutes

FEEDBACK

Paired reading

Ask the group to take out their paired reading record cards. Ask everybody to share with a partner how paired reading has been going. They should focus on both the positive and difficult issues. Use the following slide to suggest some of the questions they might think about together.

PAIRED READING

How easy has it been to do the following?

- Engage and motivate the child
- Find the right reading materials
- Find a suitable time and a comfortable space
- Use the techniques of paired reading
- Practise regularly

When each pair has finished, ask for feedback.

Advice for children who have minimal reading skills

Make sure that you address the needs of carers in the group whose children have very limited reading skills. These carers can choose a very simple picture story book to read to their child – with one short sentence to a page. They should read this to the child on a number of occasions, making sure that they talk together about the pictures and the story. In time, the child may join in some of the words or sentences, particularly if there are phrases that are repeated. It does not matter if the child is memorising bits of text.

Remind carers that they can also make a book with their child using pictures and simple text. (This was covered in Session 4 on the DVD.) Remember to keep sentences very brief – two to three words – and choose subjects that interest the child. Include high-frequency words in the child's vocabulary and lifestyle, such as names of family and friends, as well as significant places and activities. The book can be added to page by page, as and when the child is ready. Carers can tailor the book to the child's interests and abilities and this can prove a very affirming and motivating experience.

Giving praise

Ask carers to get out their home practice handouts on giving praise and to give some examples of how they used these. Find out:

HOME PRACTICE ON PRAISE

- What went well?
- What was more difficult?
- How did the child respond?

Give positive feedback where appropriate and draw out any important learning points. If carers have not been able to do the exercise, find out what has prevented them and encourage them to find ways to use praise in their everyday interactions with children.

Introduce the aims of today's session.

AIMS OF TODAY'S SESSION

- Explore the importance of self-esteem to learning
- Explore how carers can work to build children's self-esteem

20 minutes

GROUP EXERCISE

Creating a climate in which children can flourish

The impact of attitudes and behaviour on children's self-esteem

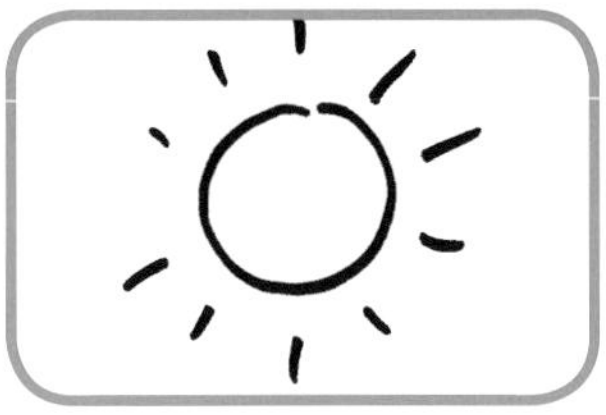

Draw a cloud and a sun on either side of your flip chart. Explain to carers that this exercise is designed to explore the impact that the child's environment can have on their self-esteem. The attitudes and behaviours of those around them can have a positive or detrimental effect on how children think and feel about themselves and on how they behave.

You will need to have prepared some post-it notes (see below).

Behaviours and attitudes

Each individual post-it note should show one of these words or terms:

- teasing
- moodiness
- inconsistency
- unresponsiveness
- giving too little responsibility
- giving too much responsibility
- being controlling
- physically distant
- no cuddles
- disapproval
- nagging
- noticing mistakes
- put-downs
- distractedness
- lecturing
- not listening
- criticism
- lack of humour
- bringing up past mistakes
- depressed
- fair rules
- negotiating
- playing together
- listening
- empathy
- laughter
- understanding
- offering choices
- humour
- cuddles
- consistency
- encouragement
- respect
- kindness
- clear boundaries
- explaining
- sharing interests
- rewards and incentives
- consequences
- ignoring minor misdemeanours

Ask each of the carers to pick up a couple of post-it notes. If the behaviour or attitude is one that is likely to encourage and affirm the child, they should place it on the sunny side of the chart. If they feel it is discouraging, they should place it on the cloudy side. There may be some discussion about where some of these behaviours or attitudes belong.

Afterwards, ask the group to think of some of the child behaviours that may result from the above experiences and write their suggestions on another flip chart sheet. Start with the behaviours that might result from living in a "cloudy" or discouraging climate. Then write up suggestions about behaviours that might result from living in a "sunny" or encouraging climate.

Examples may include:

- Living in a "cloudy" climate might result in some of the following child behaviours and attitudes: aggression, anger, isolation, bullying, boasting, stammering, coldness, whingeing, rule-breaking, disruption, rudeness, clinging, needing to please, blaming others, being a gang leader, hurtfulness, shyness, withdrawal, sickliness and so on.
- Living in a "sunny" climate might result in: co-operation, confidence, affection, friendliness, empathy, taking responsibility for actions, enthusiasm, energy, responsiveness, relaxation, appreciation and so on.

Summarise this exercise by saying that many of the children who are in foster care will have come from families who have struggled to provide nurturing care or adequate support and encouragement. In many cases, their home environment is likely to have had a detrimental effect on their self-esteem and on their behaviour and attitudes.

Refer carers to Handout 7.1, *Exploring self-esteem.*

15 minutes

GROUP EXERCISE

The origins of self-esteem

Create the space to lay out a rope along the floor of your room. At either end of the rope, place a sheet of paper or sign. One of these should show the word "terrible" and the other the word "brilliant".

Select one of the skills from the list below:

- driving
- singing
- telling jokes
- healthy eating
- DIY skills
- swimming

Carers should then position themselves at the point on the rope that reflects how good they perceive themselves to be at that particular skill.

Ask one or two people at the "terrible" end why they have rated themselves in this way. Has anyone ever told them that they were not good at this particular activity? What do they tell themselves about their abilities? Pick one or two people towards the "brilliant" end and ask the same questions.

Select two more of the skills and use this activity as the basis for a discussion about the origins of self-esteem. Where does our sense of being OK come from? Write up carers' ideas on the flip chart.

Some examples of factors which contribute to the development of self-esteem are:

- personal experience of our achievement, skill and success
- messages from others: family, teachers and friends (or what we believe they think)
- temperament/genetic disposition
- culture and community: these can positively support attributes or undervalue them.

20 minutes

QUICK-THINK

Self-esteem

There are many different ways of thinking about self-esteem, and the following slide presents just one way.

Self-esteem refers to the value we place upon ourselves. This may comprise:

SELF-ESTEEM

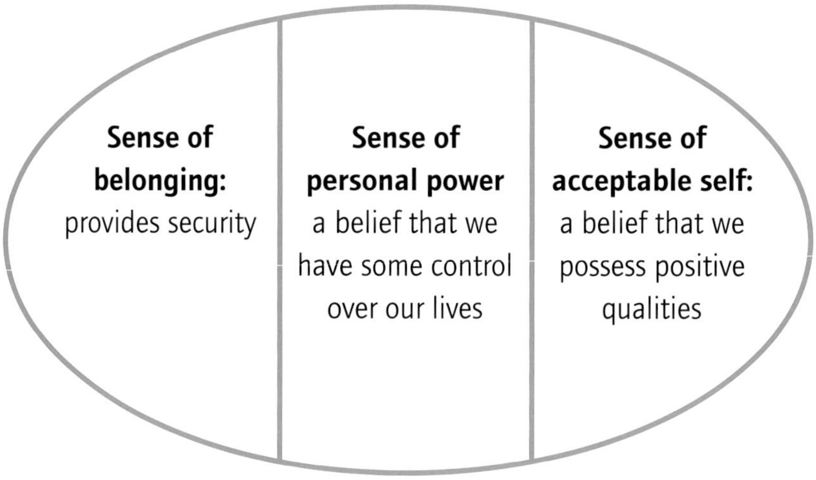
Sense of belonging: provides security
Sense of personal power a belief that we have some control over our lives
Sense of acceptable self: a belief that we possess positive qualities

Explain to the group that:

- This is a fairly simple model which suggests that self-esteem comprises three different components: a sense of belonging; a sense of personal power; and a sense of "acceptable" self (Morris and Casey, 2006).
- The development of self-esteem for children in care is not straightforward and is often compromised by the child's past experiences and by continued stress and insecurity in their lives.

Use the following three slides to help the group think about how a child might experience each of these aspects of self-esteem. Discuss carers' ideas in the group. You may want to think about particular issues that might affect a looked after child.

A SENSE OF BELONGING

- This is developed through the child's relationships with adults and peers
- It is communicated through what others say and what others do

Children in care are likely to have connections with a number of significant adults: parents, siblings, extended family members and other people. They can belong to family groups with changing membership, and being "in care" is likely to result in them becoming a member of a number of foster family groups. So "belonging" for a child in care is something that is likely to be a complex issue. Until a child is living in a permanent placement, their sense of "belonging" can be fragile. It can be challenging for carers to help children experience security and "belonging" but the importance of doing this cannot be overestimated.

A SENSE OF PERSONAL POWER

This is created through:

- Feeling that people around us notice and listen to us
- Seeing that our views have an impact on what happens in the world around us
- Having opportunities to participate and make choices

Looked after children can easily feel that they have little control in the decisions that are made about their lives, so it is especially important to find ways to enable them to experience some sense of personal "efficacy" or power.

A SENSE OF ACCEPTABLE SELF

This is created through:

- Feeling loved and cared for
- Knowing that we possess qualities that are valued by others
- Experiences of success or affirmation from others

Looked after children are separated from their families, who are the most potent and significant sources of self-esteem for most children. Children separated from their families may believe that this in itself is a reflection that they are unlovable.

The effects of self-esteem on learning

Explain to the group that self-esteem affects many areas of children's lives, and it inevitably impacts on their attitudes to learning. Use the following slides to encourage the group to reflect on the learning behaviour of the children in their care.

CHILDREN WHO HAVE GOOD SELF-ESTEEM LEARN WELL BECAUSE THEY ARE:

- Able to tolerate difficulties and uncertainty
- Able to accept praise
- Ready to try new challenges
- More likely to be optimistic and to have positive expectations of themselves and of new learning situations

CHILDREN WITH POOR SELF-ESTEEM LEARN LESS WELL BECAUSE THEY ARE LIKELY TO:

- Avoid new challenges in case they fail
- Be defensive if they feel criticised
- Be pessimistic about the chances of success and therefore give up easily
- Be prone to negative thoughts and expectations: 'I'll never be able to do that!'

10 minutes

INPUT AND DISCUSSION

THE CYCLE OF LOW SELF-ESTEEM

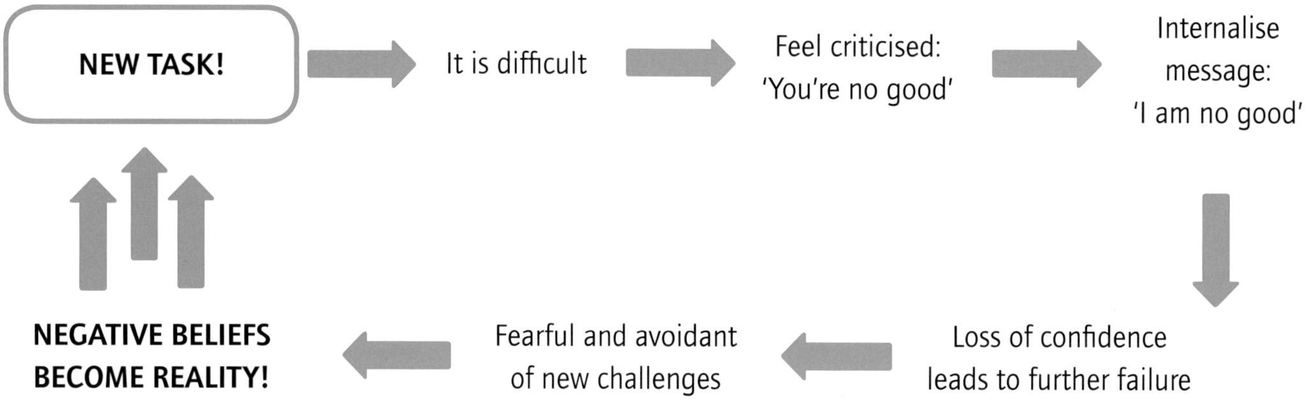

Poor self-esteem affects children's expectations of themselves and their motivation. These can easily become self-fulfilling prophecies, as the above slide demonstrates.

Ask the group if they have any examples of a child's beliefs and expectations becoming self-fulfilling prophecies.

This is shown on Handout 7.2, *The cycle of low self-esteem.*

20 minutes **BREAK**

10 minutes

INPUT

HOW I AM AND HOW I WOULD LIKE TO BE

Explain to the group that another way of thinking about self-esteem relates to how much overlap there is between "how we think we are" and "how we would like to be". Use the following slide to explore this.

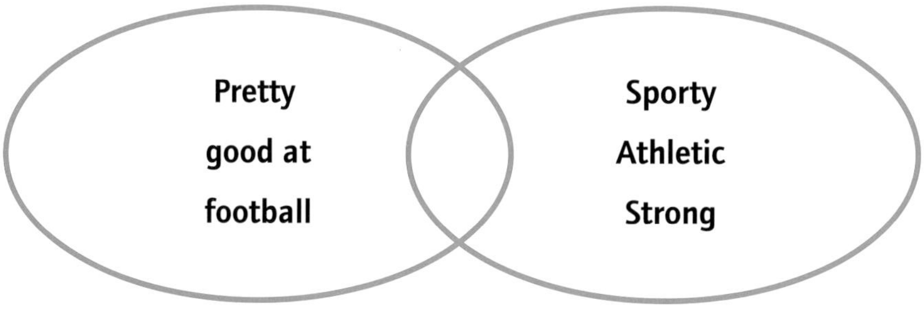

A boy who is good at football may have good self-esteem amongst his peers, if this is a skill that they value. There is a good overlap between how he sees himself and how he would ideally like to be.

PROBLEMS OCCUR WHEN CHILDREN HAVE A NEGATIVE IMAGE OF THEMSELVES AND BELIEVE THAT THEY LACK THE QUALITIES THAT OTHERS PRIZE

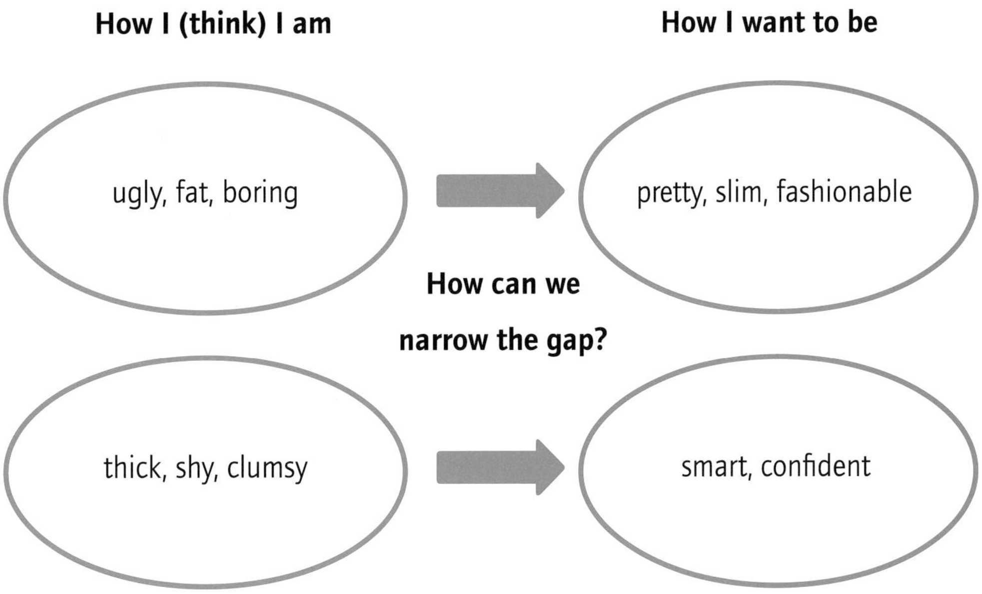

Children with low self-esteem struggle with the gap between how they believe themselves to be and how they would like to be. There are many ways of trying to address this disparity. In the next exercise, carers have the opportunity to share their experiences of helping children with poor self-esteem to think and feel more positively about themselves.

Handout 7.3, *Self-esteem,* briefly outlines the theories on self-esteem.

30 minutes

SMALL GROUPS EXERCISE

Supporting self-esteem

Draw outline of child with headings around it: "belonging" "personal power" and "sense of acceptable self", and arrows directed towards the "child". Or you can use the slide below.

SUPPORTING SELF-ESTEEM

Divide the carers into three small groups and ask them to think in their groups about the things they do to help build children's self-esteem. Carers may find it helpful to think about what they do to enhance the child's sense of "belonging", "personal power" and "acceptable self". Ask the groups to write down ideas for practical and specific actions and activities.

Draw a rough outline of a child's body on the flip chart and take feedback from each of the groups, writing their ideas inside the child's body – filling it up with activities and experiences that can improve self-esteem.

Note for trainers: ideas could include:

- **Belonging:** Explain family rules, personalise room, make sure there are photos of the child in your house, include child in family activities, involve child in family rituals, celebrate birthdays and festivals, go on trips and holidays. Do all the "normal" things a parent would do: go to parents' evening, show interest in child's interests, help the child to maintain positive links with birth family and previous care-givers, keep links with child's culture and religion, talk about people and events in child's past, use life-story resources...
- **Personal power:** Provide choices, provide opportunities for appropriate responsibility: for chores, caring for pets, etc, give pocket money, allow child to learn from their mistakes, encourage personal interests, listen to your child's views and act on these where you can, explain your and others' decisions, encourage the child to express their ideas and opinions, encourage involvement in child care reviews...
- **Acceptable self:** Provide lots of different opportunities to engage in new activities and groups, clubs and hobbies, encourage friendships. Provide loads of praise and affirmation. Notice all sorts of positive and appropriate behaviours: social skills, emotional sensitivity and understanding, intellectual and practical skills and talents.

Refer carers to Handout 7.4 *Encouraging self-esteem.*

15 minutes

STORY-TELLING

Explain to the group that we are going to spend some time thinking about story-telling.

STORY-TELLING

- Story-telling is an important social process: it is a valuable way of communicating information and values from one group to another
- It is an active process, involving the listener and the story-teller in engaging with each other
- Story-telling can be deeply healing and it is a wonderful way of sharing knowledge and wisdom

Conveying messages and values

Stories convey a whole range of different types of information, wisdom and values.

The following slide includes some well-known children's stories. Carers may be able to add to this with stories from their own particular backgrounds and culture.

CHILDREN'S STORIES

- Cinderella
- Pinocchio
- Little Red Riding Hood
- Anansi
- The Three Little Pigs

QUICK-THINK

Themes and messages

Ask carers to identify some of the themes or underlying messages that are conveyed in children's stories, using the stories on the slide as your starting point. Some examples could include: surviving neglect, growing up and learning about right and wrong, "stranger danger", surviving in a hostile world, and so on

You may want to write up some of these ideas on the flip chart.

DISCUSSION

Encouraging children to tell their own stories

It is worthwhile spending a few moments to consider the benefits of encouraging children to recount events and stories.

ENCOURAGING CHILDREN TO TELL THEIR OWN STORY

- Learning how to recount stories is an important skill for children to develop
- Talking develops cognitive and communication skills as well as confidence
- Encourage the child to tell you what has happened at school, what they have done outside the home, and so on
- Looked after children often need support to piece together and understand the story of their own lives

A key skill in life is to tell one's own story – to give an account of what has made you who you are. This sense of "personal narrative" can be particularly difficult for looked after children, who have experienced separations and multiple care-givers, and who may have undergone trauma. These children often have muddled, contradictory and disjointed ideas about their life stories. Along the way, they have lost information about themselves or have become confused about people and events. Story-telling is particularly significant for these children and they need opportunities to recount stories about themselves and their past.

5 minutes

GROUP QUICK-THINK

Good story-telling techniques

Ask carers how we go about telling stories in an engaging way. Put their ideas on the flip chart.

Examples might be:

- dramatic expression
- pacing
- using different voices
- showing pictures
- interacting with your "audience"
- getting the child to join in

20 minutes

GROUP EXERCISE

Reading a story

Select a children's story that is meaningful in terms of its emotional and social content. You could use a story such as *Ruby and the Rubbish Bin* by Margot Sunderland (Speechmark Publishing, 2003). This book is a "therapeutic story", particularly relevant to this session as it is about a girl who has low self-esteem. One day she makes a new friend at school and things begin to change.

One of the trainers can begin by reading a few pages. The aim is to have some fun and remind the group of the power of telling stories. Read with expression and relate to the group as you read – showing pictures and so on. Ask for a few volunteers to take turns to read a few pages. Be sensitive to anyone who is not comfortable with reading out loud in public.

10 minutes

HOME PRACTICE

Paired reading

Ask the carers to continue with paired reading. Provide additional paired reading record cards.

'You're special'

Ask carers to do the following, together with the child:

Cut out a photograph or draw a picture of the child to place in the centre of a sheet of paper. Then around the outside, write down or draw some of the things that you value about the child: you have a lovely smile, you are good at basketball, you are always on time to go to school, you are patient with the younger children in the house, you have a good sense of humour, and so on. Handout 7.5, *You're special*, gives an example.

5 minutes

EVALUATION

Ask carers to complete the evaluation for today's session.

5 minutes

CLOSING ROUND

Today we have been focusing largely on self-esteem as it applies to children. Of course, these ideas apply equally to ourselves, and it is important for carers to take good care of themselves and to pay attention to their own needs for esteem. The handouts on self-esteem apply to adults as well as to children. Carers may want to look at these in their own time.

Refer them to Handout 7.6, *Building your own self-esteem.* Ask carers to think of one thing that they will do in the coming week to value and look after themselves. For instance, they might want to make some time for themselves, give themselves a small treat or try to think in a positive way about themselves.

You could pass round a bowl of sweets, fruit or other small treats such as items for the bath, if this is appropriate for your group.

HANDOUT 7.1

Exploring self-esteem

creating a climate in which children can flourish

Attitudes and behaviours of others

teasing, coldness,moodiness
sending to coventry
being inconsistent, unresponsive
giving too much responsibility
giving little responsibility
being controlling
physically distant
no cuddles
disapproving, nagging
noticing mistakes, favouritism
put-downs, labelling
distracted, lecturing
not listening, critical
humourless, offering no choices
bringing up past mistakes

praise, fair rules
noticing appropriate behaviour
negotiating
playing together
listening, empathy
accepting, laughter
understanding
offering choices
humour, cuddles
consistency, encouragement
responsibility, respect
kindness, clear boundaries
explaining, sharing interests
ignoring minor misbehaviours
rewards, consequences
incentives

↓

Impact on the child's self-esteem

↓

Resulting behaviour and attitudes in the child

aggression
anger
disinterest
isolation
bullying, boasting
insecure
whingeing
breaking rules
somatising (e.g. tummyache)
disruption
rudeness and cheekiness
needing to please
clinginess, withdrawal
blaming
hurtful

co-operative
confident
affectionate
friendly and sociable
empathic and kind
takes responsibility for actions
enthusiastic
energetic
glad to please
relaxed
praises others
fun-loving

HANDOUT 7.2

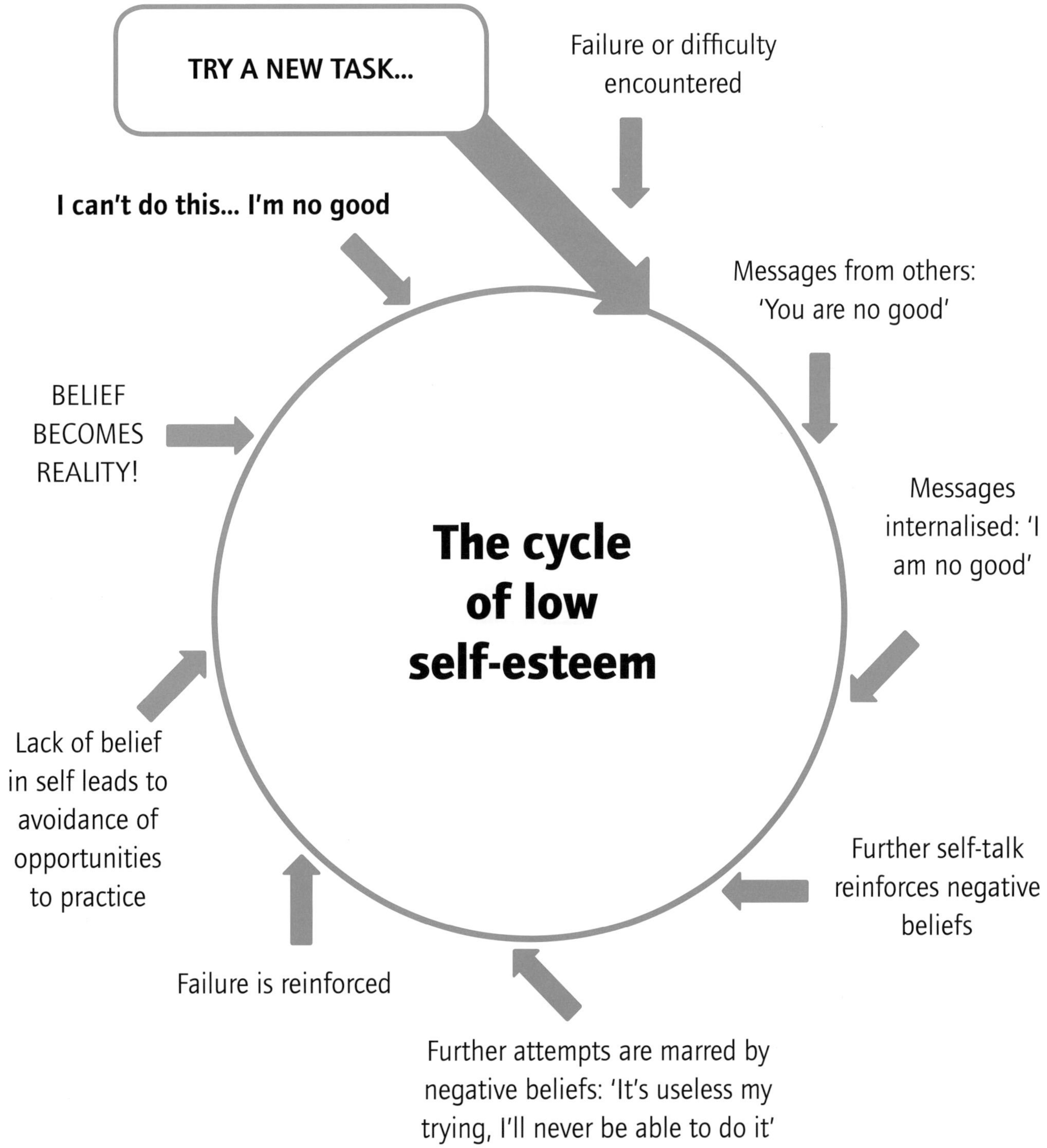
TRY A NEW TASK...
Failure or difficulty encountered
Messages from others: 'You are no good'
Messages internalised: 'I am no good'
Further self-talk reinforces negative beliefs
Further attempts are marred by negative beliefs: 'It's useless my trying, I'll never be able to do it'
Failure is reinforced
Lack of belief in self leads to avoidance of opportunities to practice
BELIEF BECOMES REALITY!
I can't do this... I'm no good
The cycle of low self-esteem

HANDOUT 7.3

Self-esteem

Self-esteem refers to the value we place upon ourselves. There are different ways of thinking about self-esteem, but one way of conceptualising it is to think of self-esteem as being made up of different components. These could include, for example:

1 **our sense of belonging** – which may be communicated in the ways others behave towards us, such as how they talk, act and relate to us

2 **our sense of personal power** – our experience of having some control over our life and of having our ideas heard and taken into account

3 **our sense of our acceptable self** – our belief that we possess qualities that we and others value positively.

Model of self-esteem

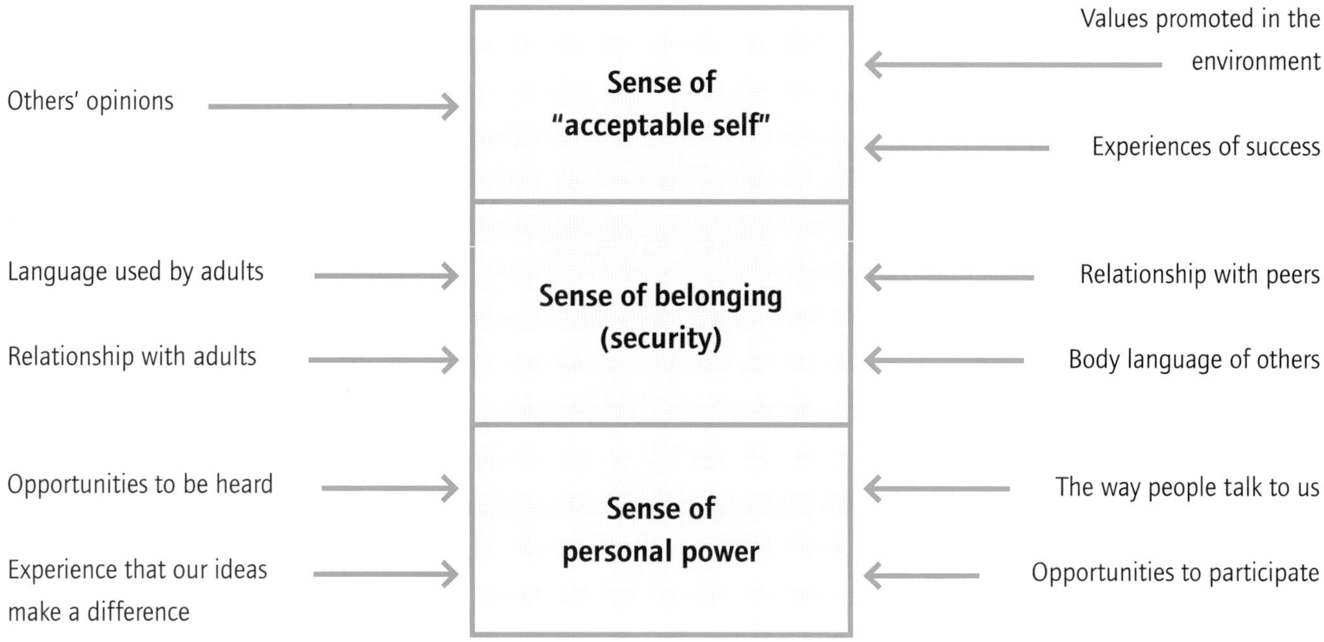

(based on Morris and Casey, 2006)

We can also think about self-esteem as reflecting the distance between what we believe ourselves to be (our self-image) and what we would like to be (our "ideal self").

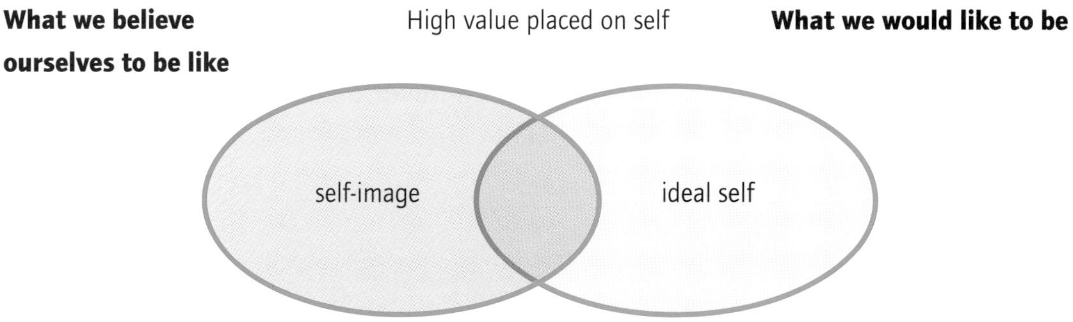

When our self-image is relatively good and our concept of "ideal self" is relatively realistic (we don't hold impossibly high expectations of ourselves), then the difference between the two is not too great and we may feel fairly positive about ourselves.

There is a big gap between how we believe ourselves to be and how we would like to be

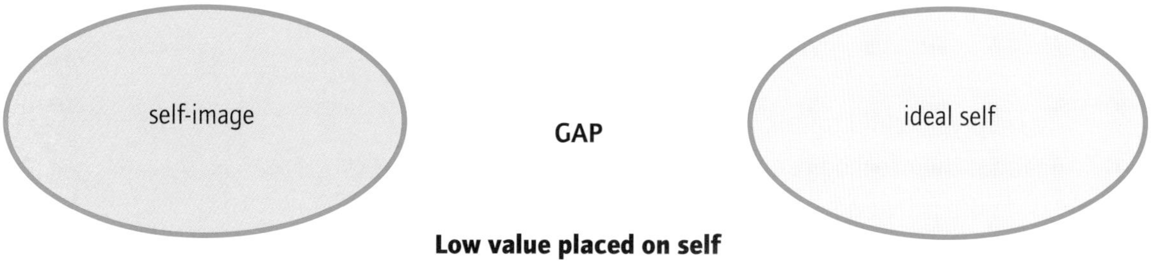

Low value placed on self

When we have a negative view of ourselves, and hold unrealistic expectations of how we should be, the distance between the two "selves" is great and the value we place on ourselves tends to be low.

One of the tasks in working with children with poor self-esteem is to help them to build a more positive image of who they are. These children need massive amounts of positive feedback to help them become more aware of their personal abilities and qualities. It may also be possible, over time, to help them to take pride in achieving small goals and improvements rather than holding rigid and unrealistic expectations of themselves.

Self-esteem exerts a powerful influence on children's learning behaviour, as it colours their beliefs and expectations about their abilities.

Children with poor self-esteem learn less well because they are:

- likely to avoid new challenges in case these invite failure
- likely to be defensive if they feel criticised
- pessimistic about the chances of success and therefore easily give up
- prone to negative thoughts and expectations: *'I'll never be able to do that!'*

Children who have good self-esteem learn well because they are:

- able to tolerate failure and criticism without falling apart
- able to accept praise
- ready to try new challenges
- more likely to be optimistic and to have positive expectations of themselves in new learning situations.

HANDOUT 7.4

Encouraging self-esteem

Praise your child's efforts and achievements: **use praise and encouragement, celebrate achievements**

Help your child to talk about their feelings and find positive ways of managing these: **show empathy, be a good role model and encourage problem-solving skills**

Let your child know that you care about them: **give positive attention and show affection**

Encourage your child to set simple goals for themselves, and to do things for themselves: **notice and reward independent actions, give responsibility**

Encourage your child to make friends: **reward pro-social behaviours and support positive social activities and friendships**

Encourage your child to express their own views and ideas and to make decisions: **show interest and respect, listen to them**

HANDOUT 7.5

Home practice: You're special

you are good at dancing
you have a lovely smile
you are always on time for school
you are patient with the other children in the house
you have a good sense of humour
you are very good at drawing

Try this activity with your child

HANDOUT 7.6

Building your own self-esteem

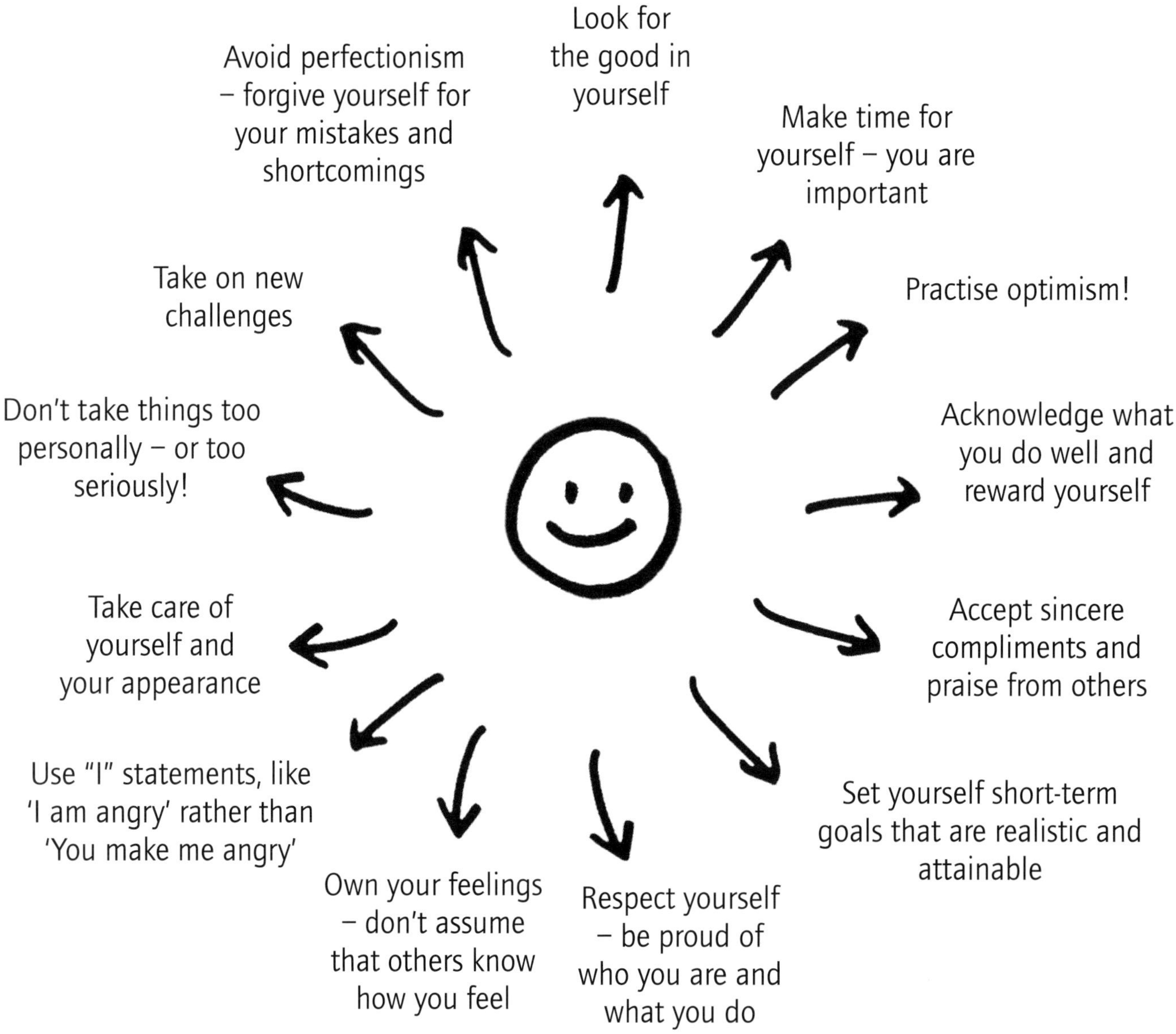
Look for the good in yourself
Make time for yourself – you are important
Practise optimism!
Acknowledge what you do well and reward yourself
Accept sincere compliments and praise from others
Set yourself short-term goals that are realistic and attainable
Respect yourself – be proud of who you are and what you do
Own your feelings – don't assume that others know how you feel
Use "I" statements, like 'I am angry' rather than 'You make me angry'
Take care of yourself and your appearance
Don't take things too personally – or too seriously!
Take on new challenges
Avoid perfectionism – forgive yourself for your mistakes and shortcomings

BE YOUR OWN BEST FRIEND!!

SESSION 8: Promoting emotional literacy

TIMETABLE

Section	Timing	Materials
1. Play music as carers arrive		CD player and music
2. Starter	**10.00–10.05**	
3. Feedback: paired reading, self-esteem Aims of the session	**10.05–10.50**	Flip chart Slide
4. Group discussion: why do we have feelings?	**10.50–11.00**	Slides Flip chart
5. Small groups exercise: identifying feelings	**11.00–11.25**	Flip chart sheets and pens for group Slide Handouts 8.1 *Identifying feelings* and 8.2 *Feelings detective posters*
6. Group quick-think: comfortable and uncomfortable feelings	**11.25–11.30**	Slide
7. Quick-think: what do we do with uncomfortable feelings?	**11.30–11.40**	Slide Flip chart
8. Small group exercise: how can we help children to manage their feelings more positively?	**11.40–12.00**	Flip chart sheets and pens Handout 8.3 *How to encourage children to talk about feelings*
9. Break	**12.00–12.20**	Refreshments
10. Quick-fire round	**12.20–12.25**	Flip chart
11. Exploring anger	**12.25–12.40**	Slides Flip chart
12. Large group exercise: cycle of arousal in anger	**12.40–1.00**	Slides Handouts 8.4 *Anger* and 8.5 *Learning about anger*
13. Avoiding angry outbursts	**1.00–1.10**	Slide
14. Small groups exercise: how can we help children to manage their anger?	**1.10–1.40**	Slide Flip chart sheets and pens Handout 8.6 *Helping children manage anger*
15. Home practice	**1.40–1.50**	Paired reading record card Handouts 8.7 *Feelings charts*, 8.8 *Books and feelings* and 8.9 *Game: knowing your feelings*

16. Evaluation	**1.50–1.55**	Evaluation form
17. Closing round	**1.55–2.00**	

Welcome carers as they arrive.

RESOURCES

CD player and music CDs (optional)
Flip chart, pens
Laptop, CD-ROM with Powerpoint presentation, projector, screen
Refreshments

HANDOUTS

Please print these from the CD-ROM supplied and give each carer a copy of the handouts for today.

8.1 *Identifying feelings*
8.2 *Feelings detective posters*
Understanding my feelings – download from: http://nationalstrategies.standards.dcsf.gov.uk/node/65930?uc=force_uj
Understanding other people's feelings – download from: http://nationalstrategies.standards.dcsf.gov.uk/node/65769?uc=force_uj
What do you do with difficult feelings?
8.3 *How to encourage children to talk about feelings*
8.4 *Anger*
8.5 *Learning about anger*
8.6 *Helping children manage anger*
Paired reading record cards
8.7 *Feelings charts*
8.8 *Books and feelings*
8.9 *Game: knowing your feelings*
Evaluation form

MUSIC: Consider playing some upbeat music at the start of this session. Music is a wonderful tool for creating mood. You will need to consider the musical and cultural preferences of your group.

Note for trainers: This session focuses on the importance of identifying and managing feelings. You may find that this opens up some personal issues for carers. If carers share information about difficult events in their own family lives, you will need to handle this sensitively. You should maintain some limits and boundaries to this discussion, but at the same time acknowledge the significance and impact of these experiences and feelings.

5 minutes

STARTER

Ask carers to share with the group what they do to calm themselves when they are feeling stressed.

45 minutes

FEEDBACK

Paired reading

Ask each carer to report back on their progress with paired reading. Ask them to talk about the things they are pleased with and the things they have struggled with. Encourage the group to give constructive feedback and find solutions to any problems.

Self-esteem

Ask carers to feed back on the "You're special" exercise. If they have brought the sheet with them, encourage them to share this and tell the group how this activity went. Provide affirmation for the work carers have done.

Introduce the aims of today's session.

AIMS OF TODAY'S SESSION

- Identify the role that feelings have in our lives
- Develop skills to help children identify and manage their feelings
- Explore what happens when we get angry
- Find ways to support children in managing their anger

Explain to the group that learning how to understand feelings is an important developmental task for children as they grow up. Today's session will focus on the role that feelings play in our lives and how we can support children to understand and manage their feelings more positively and effectively.

10 minutes

GROUP DISCUSSION

Why do we have feelings?

Ask the group what purpose they think feelings have in their lives and write up their ideas on the flip chart.

To aid this discussion, use the following slide.

FEELINGS

Feelings are like "signposts" – they provide us with valuable information about ourselves and our surroundings.

What might the following emotions signal to us?

- fear
- anger
- guilt
- happiness

Fear and anxiety may warn us of a potential threat and the need to be careful.

Anger can be a sign that something is wrong or unjust and that we need to protect ourselves, keep safe or stand up for ourselves.

Guilt indicates that we may have done something wrong and that we need to make amends.

Happiness indicates that things have gone well and that we are happy with ourselves or events.

To conclude the discussion, show the following slide.

FEELINGS

- Feelings are neither good nor bad – they provide us with important information about ourselves and the world we live in
- Feelings are not necessarily accurate indicators about ourselves or the world around us
- Some feelings are more comfortable than others
- How we understand and express our feelings can be both positive and negative for ourselves and for others

25 minutes

SMALL GROUPS EXERCISE

Identifying feelings

This exercise is designed to help carers think about some of the ways they can help children to learn about and identify feelings.

Divide carers into two or three small groups and ask them to look at Handout 8.1, *Identifying feelings*. Each group should consider one of the scenarios, listed 1 to 3 on the sheet.

Explain to the carers that you would like them to try and put themselves in the child's shoes and imagine what they might be feeling and experiencing in a particular situation. The groups will need to think about: what is going on inside the child's body; what are they thinking; what do they look like; and what do they feel like doing? Encourage the groups to be as concrete and descriptive as they can and to jot down their ideas. Each group should then feed back to the large group.

For example:

You've been fighting in the playground and you've been sent to the head teacher's office.

What's happening inside my body?	What's my face showing?	What am I thinking?	What do I feel like doing?	What's my body doing on the outside?
Heart racing Shallow, fast breathing Sweating Tight muscles	Red and hot Tight jaw Eyes staring Hard angry look	'How can I get out of this?' 'It's not fair – it wasn't my fault!' 'She won't believe me!'	Running Crying Hiding	Tense Still

To conclude this exercise, show the following slide.

IDENTIFYING FEELINGS

- All children need to learn how to understand their feelings
- Many looked after children may have missed out on opportunities to learn about their emotions
- They may be confused, detached or overwhelmed by how they feel
- Carers can help children to learn about their feelings by helping them to identify what is going on in their bodies and in their minds

Draw carers' attention to the *Feelings detective* posters on Handout 8.2. There are two posters to help children think about and identify their own and others' feelings. Some children will be familiar with these ideas and some of these resources through their schools.

5 minutes

GROUP QUICK-THINK

Comfortable and uncomfortable feelings

Explain to the group that for everybody there are some feelings that are less "comfortable" or "acceptable" than others. These feelings are often more difficult to acknowledge or to share.

Using the following slide, ask the carers to rate from 0–10 how comfortable they are in managing and expressing some of the emotions listed. Take feedback from the group and acknowledge the differences in personal response.

COMFORTABLE AND UNCOMFORTABLE FEELINGS

Uncomfortable — **Comfortable**

0 ⟵⟶ 10

Happiness, excitement, jealousy, calm, anger, shame, delight, resentment, depression, love, despair...

10 minutes

QUICK-THINK

What do we do with uncomfortable feelings?

Explain to the group that children deal with their emotional distress in very different ways depending on their needs, experiences and personalities. Some children are prone to act out and show their distress, whereas others are more likely to internalise their difficulties, keeping their feelings more to themselves.

Ask carers to think about the kinds of things children and adults do when they find it hard to openly share and express their emotions. Write up their ideas on the flip chart.

Use the following slide to prompt discussion.

UNHELPFUL WAYS OF MANAGING DIFFICULT FEELINGS

To sum up, explain to the group that although strategies like withdrawing, bottling up, acting out or "dumping" may provide relief in the short term, they often do little to constructively deal with the problem. In the longer term, they may also be damaging to the child's health and self-esteem and destructive to their relationships with others.

20 minutes

SMALL GROUP EXERCISE

How can we help children to manage their feelings more positively?

Divide the carers into two small groups and ask them to reflect on the different things they do to help the children in their care to manage their feelings. Ask them to think about ideas to help both those children who externalise their difficulties and those who internalise. Carers may come up with a mix of general principles as well as specific ideas. Ask groups to write down their ideas on a flip chart sheet.

Groups should then feed back to the large group.

Some ideas might be:

- Being physically and emotionally available when the child wants to talk
- Talking about your own feelings and modelling appropriate ways of expressing them
- Noticing the child's emotional cues and naming the feeling
- Responding to the child's state of emotional arousal and providing soothing or encouraging activity as appropriate
- Trying to help the child identify and express how they feel
- Helping the child make the links between how they feel inside, what they are thinking and how they are behaving
- Praising the child for dealing with emotions constructively
- Reminding the child that difficult feelings will pass

- Avoiding saying 'Don't cry'...'Don't get angry'...'You make me feel...'
- Not dismissing, avoiding, ignoring, denying or making light of children's feelings

Refer carers to Handout 8.3, *How to encourage children to talk about feelings.*

20 minutes **BREAK**

5 minutes

QUICK-FIRE ROUND

Go around the group and ask each carer to describe one helpful way and one unhelpful way in which they themselves express anger, writing these on the flip-chart.

15 minutes

EXPLORING ANGER

Of all the emotions that we experience, anger is for many people one of the most challenging.

Display the following slide:

ANGER

- Anger is a healthy and normal response
- It tells us how we feel about things and warns us when things feel wrong
- Anger can be expressed safely and constructively
- Children need to learn how to manage their anger
- It is OK to be angry BUT it is not OK to hurt yourself, others, or property

Children vary in what makes them angry and how they respond. Learning situations are, however, a common trigger for anger and frustration, particularly for children whose confidence, circumstances and current abilities are poor.

Explain to the group that it is helpful for children to understand what happens in their body when they are angry. Show the following slide to recap.

WHAT HAPPENS IN OUR BODIES WHEN WE FEEL ANGRY?

We may feel:
Hot, dizzy or sweaty

We may have:
A racing heart, shallow breath, dry mouth, butterflies in the stomach and tense muscles

Explain to the group that the physiological changes that take place in our bodies when we are angry are part of the "fight-flight" response.

FIGHT–FLIGHT RESPONSE

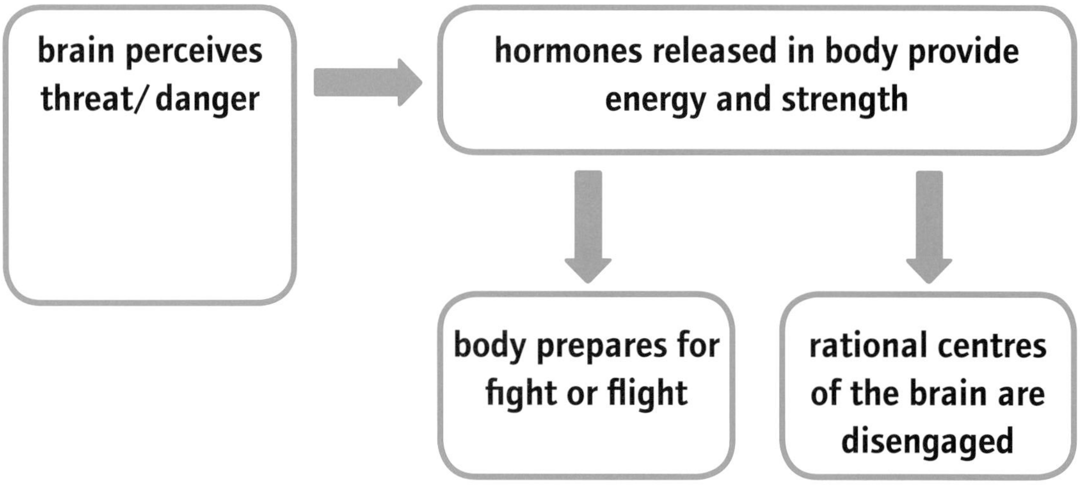

Explain the following about the fight-flight response:

- It is our body's natural response to situations where we feel threatened or in danger
- Hormones released in the body provide a burst of energy and strength and prepare the body for combat or escape
- At the same time, the rational part of the brain is temporarily disengaged – reducing our ability to judge situations and to act logically

HOW THE FIGHT–FLIGHT RESPONSE IS TRIGGERED

- In our distant past the fight-flight reflex was an adaptive response, providing protection from life-threatening dangers and ensuring survival. It was better to run first and ask questions later!
- Today we have fewer threats to life but this response still gets triggered by stress and strong emotions
- Avoiding impulsive expression of anger allows time for the "thinking" brain to engage and decide on more appropriate action

Today we face far fewer life-threatening situations and so the impulse for fight or flight is less appropriate. Nonetheless, this response still does get triggered, sometimes by a loud, unexpected noise or by situations that may pose some kind of emotional threat. Children need to be able to respond to situations that threaten and challenge them. However, they need to learn how to avoid reacting impulsively and find, instead, strategies that enable them to think and act more constructively.

20 minutes

LARGE GROUP EXERCISE

Cycle of arousal in anger

Explain to the group that we are going to explore the physiological changes that take place in our bodies when we become angry. Use the following slide to look at the cycle of bodily arousal.

ANGER: THE CYCLE OF AROUSAL

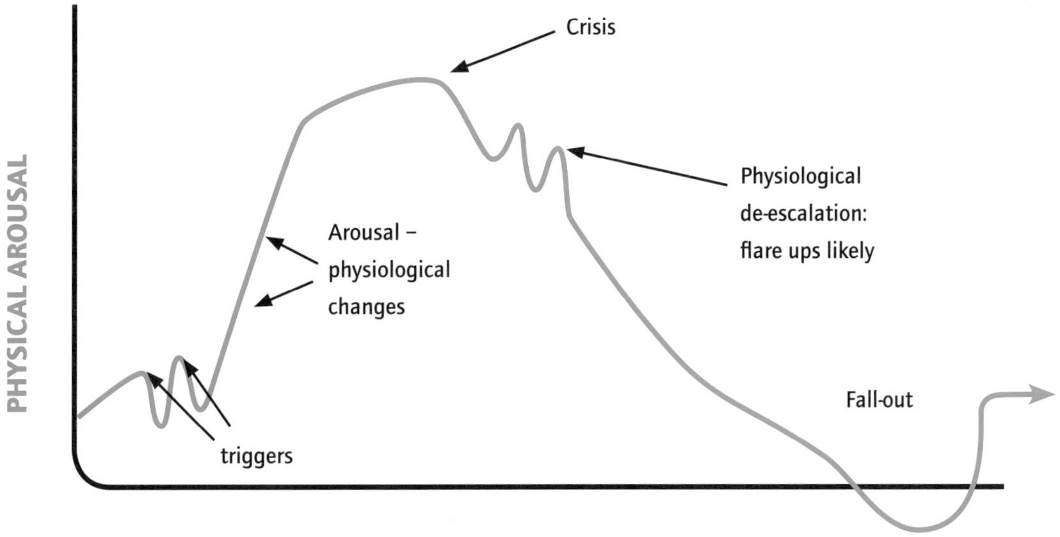

This graph shows the pattern of physiological arousal from the initial triggers through to eventual recovery. Children can benefit from learning about the bodily changes that take place as this can help them become more aware when they are becoming more angry and aroused.

Use the following slides to stimulate discussion about the different stages involved in the process of anger arousal.

1) WHAT ARE THE "TRIGGERS" THAT REGULARLY PROVOKE AN ANGRY RESPONSE FROM THE CHILD?

Ask carers to call out the things that anger the children in their care. You may want to encourage them to consider triggers that arise in relation to school, reading or learning more generally. Write these on to a flip chart.

Examples of triggers might be: not getting their own way, teasing by peers, making mistakes, not being able to understand something, competition over computer or television, mealtimes, getting over-excited, transitions from one activity to another, homework and so on.

2) WHAT ARE THE BODILY SIGNS OF AROUSAL?

Ask the carers to list the changes that take place in the body when someone becomes angry. Write these examples on a flip chart.

Examples are: sweating, dizziness, fidgetiness, increased heart rate, dry mouth, shallow quick breathing, butterflies in the stomach, clenched fists...

3) WHAT BEHAVIOURS DO WE SEE WHEN THE CHILD "EXPLODES"? WHAT FACULTIES ARE IMPAIRED AT THIS POINT?

Ask the carers to call out some examples of behaviour. Write these examples on a flip chart.

Examples might be: shouting, yelling, kicking, swearing, flailing arms, breaking things. The inability to: think or talk rationally, keep still, interact appropriately and so on.

4) WHAT AIDS RECOVERY FROM ANGER?

Ask the carers to give examples of the ways in which children recover themselves when they have had an angry outburst, or how they support them to calm down. Write these examples on the flip chart.

Examples might be: don't talk about what has happened and avoid any strong stimulation, have some quiet time, lie on the bed, time out, go outdoors, play gentle quiet music, breathe slowly, do some simple routine activity, watch fish swimming in the fish tank and so on.

Refer carers to Handouts 8.4, *Anger,* and 8.5, *Learning about anger.*

10 minutes

AVOIDING ANGRY OUTBURSTS

Explain to the carers that they can intervene at different points in the anger cycle to help children learn skills in managing their angry feelings. One particularly important skill for children to develop is the ability to delay immediate and impulsive expression of anger. Strategies that enable the child to delay responding by just a few seconds may allow time for the child to reflect on the situation and work out a better course of action.

Use the following slide of the "traffic lights" model.

TRAFFIC LIGHTS MODEL

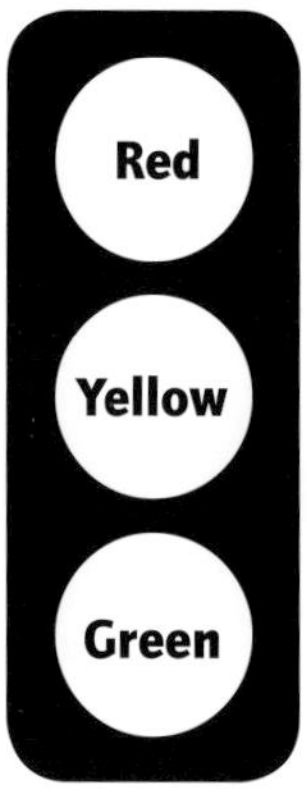

- **STOP:** when you feel provoked – just wait a few seconds and try and work out exactly what the problem is
- **THINK:** what could I do? And what would be the likely outcome if I did? Is it a good plan?
- **GO:** try something out – either now or later. Is it successful?

Ask the group whether they have any simple strategies from their experience about what children can do at the "red light" stage, the point at which they feel angry or threatened. Is there anything the child can do to buy themselves a little time and to prevent an explosion of anger?

Examples might be to: count to 10, walk away, put their hands in their pockets (to avoid hitting out), try and breathe deeply, picture something calming in their mind or have a calming phrase to recite.

It is important to remember that angry feelings often do not simply evaporate. Planning what to do and trying this out are integral parts of the process. If the child avoids taking action, the problem is unlikely to resolve and they may be left with feelings of anxiety and anger which can be damaging to their emotional and physical health and relationships.

30 minutes

SMALL GROUPS EXERCISE

How can we help children to manage their anger?

Divide carers into groups of three or four and ask them to draw on their experience to think about how they might support a child in managing their anger.

Use the following slide to provide some prompts for their discussion.

SUPPORTING CHILDREN WITH SKILLS FOR MANAGING ANGER

What strategies would you use to help the child with:

- responding to triggers
- avoiding an impulsive explosion of anger
- problem-solving after the event
- any other ideas

Carers might think about strategies to manage the very early stages of the anger cycle, or focus on what to do at the point of crisis or during the "fall-out" period. They may even think about strategies to support the child long after the event when they are feeling quite calm. Ideas will vary depending on the age and the emotional development of the child.

Ask groups to write down their ideas on a sheet of flip chart paper. Take feedback from each group.

Practical strategies for managing anger might include:

- go for a walk
- stroke an animal
- count to 10
- relax in a hot bath
- try slow, deep breathing
- play/listen to music
- write it out
- run
- acknowledge the events and feelings leading up to feeling angry
- dance
- think of something funny
- draw a picture
- thump a pillow
- stomp
- dig the garden
- talk about it to someone supportive
- knead dough or playdough
- scream
- take time out
- have a hug
- have a cry

Note for trainers:
Ideas to hold in mind:

- Carers have an important role in helping children to understand anger. This may involve acknowledging, naming and exploring feelings. This needs to be done at times when the child is feeling calm and open to reflection.
- There are other strategies to help the child express and let go of feelings, which could be useful at times when the child is more in touch with their feelings. Some children may be responsive to drawing a picture of their angry feelings, writing them down or acting them out with puppets, for example.
- There are also strategies to relax and distract, which may help some children learn how to remain calm and avoid angry outbursts.
- Ultimately, children also need to learn how to problem-solve: to identify why they are angry, clarify how they want things to be different in the future, and think about what they could do to achieve this successfully.

Refer carers to Handout 8.6, *Helping children manage anger.*

10 minutes

HOME PRACTICE

Paired reading

Continue paired reading (provide paired reading record cards).

Exploring feelings with the child

Refer to the *Feelings charts* in Handout 8.7. There are two of these: one simple chart for use with younger children and a more detailed chart to use with older children. Ask carers to use the feelings chart each day with their children. The carer selects a feeling from the chart, points to this and tells the child about something that has happened during the day and how they felt about it. For example: 'I felt really happy this afternoon because I baked a delicious lemon cake.' OR 'I felt really sad because I broke the lovely green vase when I was cleaning this morning.'

The carer should then ask their child to pick a feeling of their own from the chart and tell the carer how that applies to something that has happened during their day. Ask carers to make notes on this "feelings dialogue" to bring back next week.

There are other resources with explanatory notes for carers in their handouts. See Handout 8.8, *Books and feelings,* and Handout 8.9, *Game: knowing your feelings.*

5 minutes

EVALUATION

Ask carers to complete the evaluation for today's session.

5 minutes

CLOSING ROUND

Ask carers to name one thing they are going to do this week which will make them feel happy.

You could play some upbeat music as carers leave.

HANDOUT 8.1

Identifying feelings

	What's happening inside my body?	What is my face showing?	What am I thinking?	What do I feel like doing?	What's my body doing on the outside?
1. You've been fighting in the playground and you've been sent to the head teacher's office					
2. You're going to sit an exam today to see if you can get into the school your mum/carer really wants you to go to and where your friends are going					
3. You've won a dance competition and you and two other children are going to the BBC to be in a children's television programme					

HANDOUT 8.2

Feelings detective posters

(http://nationalstrategies.standards.dcsf.gov.uk/primary)

Two posters supporting children when trying to recognise their own feelings. The posters are part of Social and Emotional Aspects of Learning for primary schools (SEAL) resources.

Feelings detective: understanding my feelings can be downloaded from: http://nationalstrategies.standards.dcsf.gov.uk/node/65930

Feeling detective: understanding other people's feelings can be downloaded from: http://nationalstrategies.standards.dcsf.gov.uk/node/65769

HANDOUT 8.3

How to encourage children to talk about feelings

Model discussion and expression of feelings

Don't say, 'Don't cry...don't get angry...'

Use a wide emotional vocabulary

Be accepting of the child's emotional state

Treat feelings as "normal"!

Be there if the child wants to talk

Help the child to identify feelings

Try to elicit how the child feels – don't tell them

Help the child to make the links between how they look, how they feel inside and what they feel like doing

Discourage the child from thinking that others are in control of their emotions. Avoid saying, 'You make me feel...'

Give time to talk and think about emotions

Remind the child that difficult feelings will pass

Praise the child for dealing with feelings constructively

HANDOUT 8.4

Anger

Anger is a powerful and sometimes difficult emotion which is aroused in response to threat. It is part of the self-protective fight-flight reaction. It sets off a rush of adrenaline which may be useful for responding to major life threats but which is not always so helpful for dealing with emotional hurts and challenges.

Sometimes our anger can catch us unawares, but very often we are at least partly conscious of the build-up of frustration and aggression and sometimes we can trace this back to the events which provoked us. On occasion, we may realise after the event that we overreacted or misconstrued the situation.

The pattern of arousal throughout the anger cycle

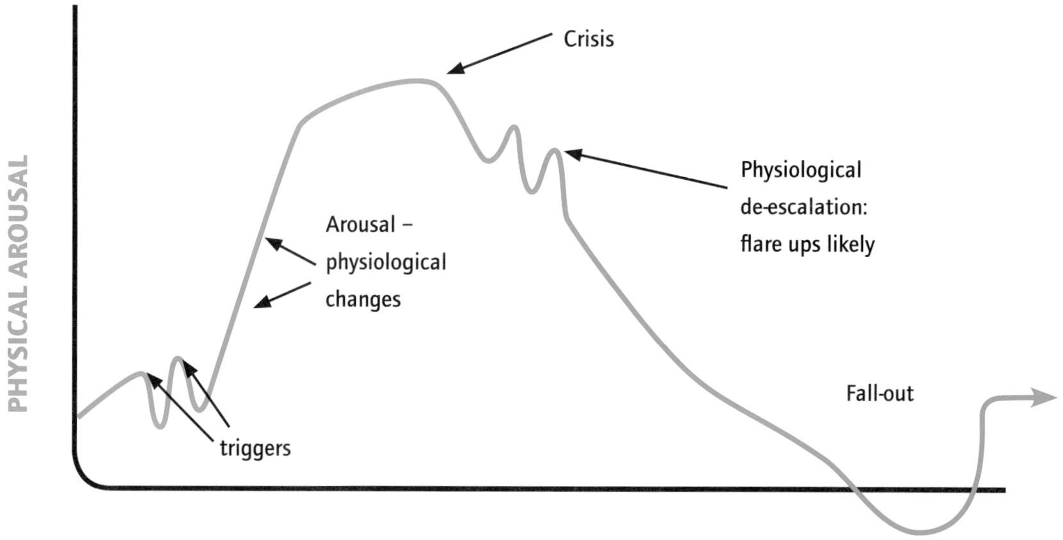

Learning about anger

It is useful to coach children about the different stages of the anger cycle and the changes that take place in their bodies. This may enable them to be more aware of situations where they become angry and help them to develop greater control. Children will benefit from learning about:

- the triggers that regularly provoke their anger
- the bodily signs of physiological arousal as well as the thoughts and feelings that accompany the experience of anger
- the loss of rational thinking that occurs when they lose their temper, and that this makes it difficult to see others' points of view, hear what they are saying or consider the consequences of their actions
- the heightened level of arousal that lasts for around 45 minutes, during which they may remain prone to "flare-ups"
- the "fall-out" period when they may feel quite low before their body returns to normal

HANDOUT 8.5

Learning about anger

Triggers
- frustration
- disappointment
- fear
- threats to personal security
- feelings of powerlessness
- being hurt by others
- rejection

Physical signs
- clenched teeth
- headache
- butterflies in tummy
- rapid heart rate
- sweaty palms
- hot neck/face
- shaking or trembling
- dizziness

Feelings
- irritation
- sadness
- guilt
- resentment
- anxiety
- aggression
- fear

Behaviours
- rubbing your head
- cupping your fist with your other hand
- pacing
- being sarcastic
- loss of humour
- raising your voice

Thoughts
- No-one loves me
- I'm a loser
- I always get the blame
- People take advantage of me
- No one respects me
- This isn't fair
- Everyone is out to get me

HANDOUT 8.6

Helping children manage anger

Many people have problems with anger because they are afraid of it. Anger may be associated with losing control, social disapproval and violence.

It is important to help children understand that anger can be a positive emotion and that it can be expressed safely and constructively. Children do need your help to learn how to do this.

Key ideas

- Anger is OK – it is a healthy and normal feeling
- Children need to learn how to express anger in constructive ways
- When expressed appropriately, anger can help to protect and motivate us
- When anger is bottled up, it can lead to depression or aggression and this is bad for our health
- Children with good self-esteem will have less need to be angry
- Learning what triggers our anger will help make it easier to control
- Being aware of our feelings helps to reduce conflict
- Anger is often bound up with feelings of hurt, fear and powerlessness
- Good listening can help to dissipate anger and improve self-esteem
- Children learn how to behave from observing how adults behave – we are their role models

Remember

- Children need to learn safe limits to their behaviour for their own security and well-being as well as that of others. They also need to know that their feelings are understood.
- Children need help to learn how to control their anger. They may need you to say "stop" firmly and to keep calm when they are starting to become aroused.
- None of us think clearly when we are angry. With children it may be best to say something like, 'We'll talk about this when you are feeling calmer.'
- Don't make the child apologise when they are not feeling sorry as this may encourage them to bury their anger and to act falsely.

When children feel threatened or frightened they may react with anger. The following are some thoughts which might arouse anger:

- I might not be loved or lovable
- I might not be safe

- I might be powerless
- I might not know what is going to happen to me
- I might not know when I will see the ones I love
- I might lose the things that are important to me
- I might not know who I can trust
- I might not belong – to family, peer group or culture
- I might be shown up and found to be not good enough
- I might not understand the rules
- I might get hurt
- I might not have anyone to talk to
- I might not know what I'm supposed to do

Different ways of helping with angry feelings

Understanding:

- Talk with the child about anger
- Talk about words for different feelings
- Encourage them to acknowledge the things that have made them angry
- Discuss triggers for anger, bodily signs, and outward behaviours
- Discuss what helps them to calm down and recover
- Work out strategies for keeping calm and avoiding outbursts
- Identify positive ways of expressing anger
- Model safe expression of angry feelings – non-blaming, assertive and constructive

Containing:

- Have rules about how to express anger safely and constructively
- Use time out or "calm-down" time to reflect and be quiet at times of conflict and anger

Therapeutic:

- Use creative activities to enable the child to express their anger, such as paint, drawing, puppets and play-dough or ripping up newspaper for papier-mâché
- Draw a shield and get the child to decorate this with things that help them to feel safe and happy

Strategies for you and the child

- **Relaxation, for example, breathing down the tension**
  Picture a 10-point scale on a thermometer and think about how angry you are. Take in a deep breath and breathe slowly out, imaging the anger coming down your tension scale. Keep breathing in and out slowly, visualising the decreasing anger, until you feel safe. Congratulate yourself.

- **Do something different**
  For instance, put your hands in your pockets instead of hitting out or throwing things.

- **Use "I" statements**
  An assertive way of expressing your feelings is to use a statement like this: 'I feel... (angry, furious, niggled), when... (say what happens), because... (why it upsets you), I would like... (what you would like to be different).'

- **Break the chain of negative, angry thoughts**
  Prepare something positive and calming to say to yourself, such as: 'Breathe slowly, keep calm, just walk away. You can do it!'
- **Think of calm things to say and do when other people sound angry with you**
  For instance: 'Mmmm, I hadn't thought of it like that', 'You may be right', 'Does that bother you?'
- **Niggles jar**
  Write down everyday things that annoy and anger you and put them into the jar.
- **Problem-solving**
  Help the child to identify what they are angry about, to clarify what they would like to happen in future, and to think about and decide what they might do to achieve that.
- **Ways to calm down**
  Count to 10, stroke an animal, think of something funny, thump a pillow, run, dig the garden, talk to someone supportive, knead dough/play-dough, play/listen to music, scream, write it out, scribble, do a relaxation exercise, have a bath...

HANDOUT 8.7a

Feelings charts

Angry

Happy

Sad

Frightened

Surprised

Disgusted

HANDOUT 8.7b

Feelings charts

Angry

Bored

Confident

Confused

Disappointed

Disapproving

Disbelieving

Disgusted

Enraged

Exasperated

Frustrated

Guilty

Happy

Hurt

Jealous

Lonely

Miserable

Negative

Nervous

Optimistic

Sad

Sympathetic

Undecided

Withdrawn

HANDOUT 8.8

Books and feelings

Choose one of your favourite story books. Read it together and look at the pictures. Think about how the characters in the book might be feeling. How many feelings can you think of?

You might want to write down some of the feelings or draw a picture. Have you ever felt the same as the characters in the book?

Feeling	A time when you have felt like that

HANDOUT 8.9

GAME: Knowing your feelings

Cut out the feelings cards and play this game with the child. Take it in turns to pick a card and say one thing that you think makes the other person feel that way. If you are the carer and you pick the relaxed card, you should say what you think makes the child relaxed. The child should then say if you got this right. If not, they should say something that does make them feel relaxed.

happy	**angry**	**sad**	**scared**
jealous	**surprised**	**excited**	**worried**
relaxed	**delighted**	**pleased**	**calm**
frustrated	**proud**	**stressed**	**guilty**

SESSION 9: Listening skills

TIMETABLE

Section	Timing	Materials
1. Play music as carers arrive		CD player and music
2. Starter: music for different moods	**10.00–10.05**	
3. Feedback: paired reading and talking about feelings Aims of the session	**10.05–10.50**	Flip chart Slide
4. Components of communication	**10.50–11.05**	Slides
5. Pairs exercise: mirroring	**11.05–11.15**	
6. Group discussion: what are the benefits of good listening?	**11.15–11.25**	Flip chart
7. Small groups discussion: what are the barriers to listening?	**11.25–11.45**	Flip chart
8. Role play: poor listening	**11.45–12.05**	Slide Handout 9.1 *Scenarios: poor listening*
9. Break	**12.05–12.25**	Refreshments
10. Small groups exercise: guidelines for good listening	**12.25–12.50**	Slide Flip chart and pens Handout 9.2 *Good listening skills*
11. Additional techniques	**12.50–1.10**	Slides Flip chart
12. Practice in pairs: listening skills	**1.10–1.40**	Handout 9.3 *Scenarios: listening skills*
13. Home practice	**1.40–1.50**	Handout 9.4 *Home practice: reflective listening* and Paired reading record cards
14. Evaluation	**1.50–1.55**	Evaluation form
15. Closing round	**1.55–2.00**	Optional treats

Welcome carers as they arrive.

RESOURCES

CD player and music CDs (optional)
Flip chart, pens
Laptop, CD-ROM with Powerpoint presentation, projector, screen
Scenarios for role play
Refreshments
Optional treats for closing round

PREPARATION

You may want to ask one of the carers in advance if they are willing to take part in the role play on "poor listening". Give them a copy of the scenarios so that they can see what is involved. Otherwise the two co-trainers can undertake this role play together.

HANDOUTS

Please print off handouts from the CD-ROM supplied and give each carer a copy of the handouts for today.

9.1 *Scenarios: poor listening*
9.2 *Good listening skills*
9.3 *Scenarios: listening skills*
9.4 *Home practice: reflective listening*
Paired reading record cards
Evaluation form

5 minutes

STARTER

Music for different moods

Ask each carer to describe the kind of music they listen to when they want to relax. You could have a second round where carers describe the music they listen to if they want to feel uplifted or energised.

45 minutes

FEEDBACK

Paired reading

Find out from each of the carers how the paired reading is going. Ask about their progress as well as any difficulties.

Talking about feelings

Find out how carers got on talking about feelings with children this week.

- Did this make any difference to their communication?
- Do they have any observations or feedback to share?

Encourage the group to continue to find ways to bring feelings into their conversations with children.

Introduce the aim of today's session.

AIM OF TODAY'S SESSION

- To enhance our listening skills

15 minutes

COMPONENTS OF COMMUNICATION

Explain to the group that you are going to begin today's session by thinking about how we communicate. Face-to-face communication involves much more than words. Use the following slides to explore the different aspects of communication and ask the group to guess what percentage of any communication is conveyed through each one.

THE COMPONENTS OF COMMUNICATION

When we communicate, we convey messages in different ways.

There are three main components to our communication. These are:

- verbal
- non-verbal
- para-verbal

Ask the group to clarify and define each of these aspects of communication.

1) Verbal communication

For example:

Verbal communication refers to the content of what we say – how we arrange the words and the meaning of the words we choose

2) Non-verbal communication

For example:

Non-verbal communication refers to, for example:

- body posture and gesture
- physical distance
- facial expression, for example, our eyes may convey excitement, worry or interest, etc.

NON-VERBAL COMMUNICATION

3) Para-verbal communication

Use the following slide:

PARA-VERBAL COMMUNICATION IS:
How we say something – the tone, pitch, pace, volume or emphasis of our voice.

For example: **I** didn't say you were stupid

I **didn't** say you were stupid

I didn't say you were **stupid**

Explore with the group how our speech can easily convey entirely different meanings. With the same words we can communicate praise or criticism, sarcasm or enthusiasm by varying the tone, pitch, pace and volume of our voice. We can give very different messages by emphasising different parts of a sentence, as the example demonstrates.

Summarise the discussion by using the following slide:

OUR FACES AND BODIES ARE POWERFUL COMMUNICATORS
How we say something also has a massive impact on the messages we convey.

- Non-verbal cues account for 55 per cent of any communication
- Para-verbal cues account for 38 per cent
- Verbal content of what we say accounts for 7 per cent

When we communicate with children, we need to remember that how we express ourselves is at least as important as our actual words, if not more so. In the same way, when children communicate with us, much of the meaning of their message will be embedded in their non-verbal and para-verbal cues. Good listening involves paying attention to these underlying messages.

10 minutes

PAIRS EXERCISE

Mirroring

Explain to the group that listening is about relating to the other person in their entirety – noticing and attending to the non-verbal messages as well as the verbal ones. This exercise will give carers an experience of tuning in to another person at a non-verbal level.

Ask carers to get into pairs and to sit or stand opposite each other. They are to imagine that they are looking in a mirror. One person takes the lead and in their own time makes different faces and gestures while their partner physically mirrors or copies them. If carers feel uncomfortable making faces, they can pretend to comb their hair, play a violin or put their make-up on, for example. After a couple of minutes, ask carers to swap roles.

Take feedback from the group.

- How did this feel?
- What did carers notice?
- Did they feel that their mirroring skills improved?

10 minutes

GROUP DISCUSSION

What are the benefits of good listening?

Listening is a key skill. Using the flip chart to record their ideas, think with the group about the advantages of good listening: what are the beneficial outcomes for both children and adults when we listen attentively?

Note for trainers:

Ideas could include:

Listening enables us to understand the world of the child.

It can help us to understand:

- how the child feels
- how the child interprets and understands what is going on around them
- what the child finds difficult

Listening also helps the child to feel:

- less isolated
- more calm and supported.

It may provide the opportunity for:

- greater closeness and intimacy
- development of self-expression, self-understanding, problem-solving, etc.

20 minutes

SMALL GROUPS DISCUSSION

What are the barriers to listening?

Explain that, although most people really appreciate being listened to, listening is not always a natural or easy thing to do. In the home, there are many different things that can get in the way of our listening attentively to children.

Ask carers to discuss in groups of three some of the factors that can make it difficult to notice or respond to what children might be trying to say.

Take feedback in the large group and write carers' ideas on the flip chart.

Note for trainers:

Possible factors may be:

- finding the subject matter painful
- feeling burdened by other responsibilities
- feeling tired
- not understanding
- feeling that we have heard it all before
- fear that talking may increase the child's distress
- anxiety about not knowing the answers or not knowing what to do or say
- being preoccupied with our own experiences, issues and worries
- lack of empathy
- lack of time
- not liking or feeling sympathetic towards a child

20 minutes

ROLE PLAY

Poor listening

Explain to the group that good listening involves responding to the underlying emotional messages as well as hearing the words. Before we move on to explore good listening, we want to consider in a little more detail those times when we fail to acknowledge the emotional content of what children say.

Use Handout 9.1, *Scenarios: poor listening,* which provides four short dialogues. These demonstrate how adults sometimes fail to respond to the emotional content of children's communications.

Choose two or three of the scenarios to enact in front of the group. You will need to involve both of the trainers, or you might recruit one of the carers at the beginning of the session to play the part of the child.

Explain to the carers that they are going to observe some everyday interactions between a child and their carer, in which the child is experiencing a degree of distress. Explain to the group that you want them to identify what is going on in each situation. Does the adult empathise with the child's feelings? If not, what do they do instead?

SCENARIO 1

Explain that this scenario takes place when the child comes home from school.

Child: (Sad, disappointed and downcast) *This week I only got 2 out of 10 in the spelling test. That's even worse than last week!*

Adult: *Well, I can't say that I'm altogether surprised! You'll have to work a load harder if you want to get 10 out of 10!*

Child: (Says nothing, but hangs his head down)

Ask the group what they observed. What is the child feeling and what does the adult do?

Note to trainers: What the adult says in this scenario may in fact be true – but rather than responding to the child's sadness and disappointment, the response is critical and blaming.

SCENARIO 2

Explain to the group that in this scenario the child is trying to practise their six times table for school and reciting them to her carer but keeps on making mistakes.

Carer: *That's wrong. Think about it, and try again.*

Child: (Child is finding this very hard. She speaks slowly and unsurely, screws up eyes as she does so) *1 x 6 = 6, 2 x 6 = 12, 3 x 6 = 24, 4 x 6...*

Carer: *No, hold on a moment. You got one wrong. Just concentrate. Do it again.*

Child: (Getting very frustrated. Can't think how to do it. Grunts and mutters) *I can't do this! This is too difficult – I can't remember it. I'm no good!*

Carer: *Come on. Don't make a fuss. This is easy.* (Adult start reciting), *1 x 6 is 6, 2 x 6 is...*

Child: (Becomes very quiet and subdued. Sits there, eyes downcast, not doing anything)

Ask the group what they observed. What do they think the child is feeling and how does the adult respond to this?

In the scenario above, the child's experience and feelings are discounted or denied. This can be extremely hurtful and de-motivating.

SCENARIO 3

Child comes home from school looking unhappy.

Carer: *Hello. Oooh, what's up?*

Child: *I had a rotten day. I don't like Angus any more. He went off with my new football at play-time and he's probably gone and lost it! I hate him!*

Carer: *That's awful! Well, I'll tell you what you need to do. When you go in tomorrow morning, you say to him that if he doesn't give you back your football straight away, I'm going to come and see the teacher. And he won't be getting an invitation to your birthday party next month, will he?*

Child: (Quietly) *Look, it doesn't matter that much, honestly.*

Ask the group what they think the child is feeling and what it is that the adult does in this situation.

The carer in this scenario is desperate to put things right and jumps in very quickly to give advice. This allows little space for the child to talk about what was happening and how they felt about it all. There is also no opportunity for the child to do their own thinking about what action they want to take.

SCENARIO 4

In this scenario the child comes home from school.

Child: (Cross and upset) *Mrs Brown was horrid to me today. She yelled at me, and I felt like crying. But I didn't let anyone see.*

Carer: *What on earth did you do wrong?*

Child: (A bit downcast) *She said I was putting Michael off his work.*

Carer: *What did she say?*

Child: *Can't remember.*

Carer: *Did you get your name on the "naughty" side of the board?*

Child: *I guess.*

Carer: *Will you get detention?*

Child: *I don't know.*

Carer: *Was that the only time you got in trouble today?*

Child: (Shrugs and turns away)

Ask the group what they think the child was feeling and then to comment on what the adult does in this situation.

The adult in this scenario asks lots of questions and follows their own agenda rather than listening to what the child wants to say. This denies the child the opportunity to share their experience and what it meant to them. Again the child misses out on the opportunity to process what happened themselves and evaluate their actions for themselves.

To summarise:

- Listening and attending to a child's experiences and feelings provides a valuable opportunity to learn about the child and how they feel and think about the events in their life
- It enables the adult to connect with the child and to help the child develop a deeper understanding of themselves and the world
- It provides a shared moment of intimacy and the deepening of bonds of affection

20 minutes **BREAK**

25 minutes

SMALL GROUPS EXERCISE

Guidelines for good listening

Explain to the group that we will now explore what is involved in good listening skills.

Create two small groups and ask carers to create some guidelines or a "tip sheet" for good listening. What are the essential components of good, attentive listening? Carers may want to draw on their own experiences of being listened to or reflect on times when they feel they have been able to listen successfully to their children.

Suggest to the groups that they address the questions on the following slide:

GUIDELINES FOR GOOD LISTENING

- What are the attitudes or qualities of the listener?
- What do they say?
- What do they do?

Take feedback in the large group. Allow time for clarification and discussion.

Note to trainers: You may want to make sure that you cover some of the following points. Attentive listening requires that you:

- stop what you are doing
- listen with full attention
- listen with your "whole body"
- let the child do the talking

Refer carers to Handout 9.2, *Good listening skills*, for further details.

20 minutes

ADDITIONAL TECHNIQUES

Explain to the group that, when we listen attentively to children, we validate their experiences and help them to feel more supported and understood. Our empathy and understanding may enable the child to feel more comfortable with themselves and enhance their self-understanding. Use the following slide to discuss some of the specific skills carers can use when listening to their children.

ACKNOWLEDGING AND NAMING FEELINGS

- Many children will not be able to identify or understand what they feel
- Carers may need to "name" the feeling for them
- This will enable the child to make better sense of events and their feelings about them

Allowing the child space to feel and express an emotion, rather than moving them along quickly to something else, can be a valuable way of validating their experience and developing their emotional understanding. Many children will not know how to identify what it is that they are feeling and so they may need their carer to actually "name" it for them. For example, a carer might say 'You sound really cross about what your friend did' or 'It's disappointing when you don't get picked for the team'. Linking words with experiences and feelings builds the child's emotional vocabulary and enables them to make sense of situations and their responses to them. This is vital for social and emotional development.

Ask carers to give some examples of situations where they might be able to "name feelings" to help their child.

QUESTIONS:

- open-ended questions
- why? questions
- closed questions

Discuss with the group the impact of different types of questions.

Questions can be useful when you are talking with a child as they can convey interest and enable the child to explore their concerns more fully. Too many questions or the wrong kind of questions can be inhibiting and can even feel like being interrogated.

Open-ended questions are often the most helpful as they don't imply a wrong or right answer, but rather provide an opportunity for the child to express their viewpoint. Examples of this might be, 'You look angry – what happened?', 'You're late. What's up?', 'What you are doing is dangerous. What's going on?'

"Why...?" questions are often inhibiting as they may be experienced as critical or blaming. Children often do not know the answer to "why" questions and are at a loss how to respond. Try to avoid asking "why".

Closed questions are ones that have a "yes" or "no" answer. These are best avoided unless you have a very shy or guarded child who won't risk more than a one-word answer. Useful closed questions could be: 'Do you need my help?', 'Shall I go through that once again?'

REFLECTING BACK

- mirroring back to the child what they have said
- reflecting both feelings and actions
- being non-judgemental

Explain that one useful technique when listening is to repeat back to the child what you understand them to be saying. This is a kind of mirroring of their thoughts and feelings. It is important to be as accurate as you can, describing actions and naming feelings without judging them as "positive" or "negative".

You might say, 'It seems that you...', 'That sounds as if...', 'As you see it...'

Find out from the group whether this is a skill that they use. Allow space for discussion and reflection.

Paraphrasing can help to deepen the child's understanding of what has happened and how they feel, but the adult needs to do this in a spirit of curiosity, almost as if they are checking out with the child whether they have understood their situation and feelings correctly. It is important that the child feels able to correct the adult if they have not understood things exactly.

This may be an opportunity for trainers or group members to share and discuss other skills that they use to enable children to talk.

30 minutes

PRACTICE IN PAIRS

Listening skills

Provide Handout 9.3, *Scenarios: listening skills.* Put carers into pairs and assign each pair one of the scenarios to start work on. The carer playing the role of the child needs to imagine how the child might feel and act and convey this in the exercise with their partner. The other carer is to practise their empathic listening skills and see if they can enable the "child" to talk about what has happened, using some of the skills that have been discussed.

Encourage carers to give each other feedback – you could suggest that they tell each other anything that was helpful and one thing they might do differently.

Carers are then to swap roles and choose a second scenario.

Take feedback in the large group. Ask the carers what it felt like to be the "child" and what things they found helpful and unhelpful. Then ask how carers felt about being in the "listener" role. What did they feel comfortable with and what did they find more difficult?

10 minutes

HOME PRACTICE

Paired reading

Carers should continue with paired reading. Provide paired reading record cards where needed.

Listening skills

Ask carers to use an opportunity to listen to the child this week. One option is to talk with the child about their day at school and see what they can learn about the child's feelings and experiences. There may, of course, be some other pressing issue in the child's life and the carer may want to use their listening skills to relate to this. Ask carers to try out at least one of the skills that have been discussed today and to use Handout 9.4, *Home practice: reflective listening,* to record how they get on.

5 minutes

EVALUATION

Ask carers to complete an evaluation for the session.

5 minutes

CLOSING ROUND

Listening can be hard work. Ask carers to say one thing that they are going to do this week to reward and look after themselves. Encourage them to commit to doing something – small plans are often more manageable and achievable than grand plans. Some examples are: enjoying a relaxing scented bath, going for a walk/run, having your hair/nails done, watching the football or a DVD, reading a newspaper or magazine, having a special meal, phoning or seeing a friend, etc.

If you like, give out some small rewards at the end of the session, such as bath balls, chocolate or fruit.

HANDOUT 9.1

SCENARIOS: Poor listening

SCENARIO 1

Child comes home from school looking fed up.

Child: (Sad and disappointed) *This week I only got 2 out of 10 in the spelling test. That's even worse than last week!*

Adult: *I can't say that I'm altogether surprised! You'll have to work a load harder if you want to get 10 out of 10!*

Child: (Says nothing, but hangs his head)

SCENARIO 2

Child is trying to learn the six times table for school. She keeps making mistakes.

Carer: *That's wrong. Think about it and try again.*

Child: (Child is finding this very hard. She speaks slowly and hesitatingly, screwing up eyes) *One times six is six, two times six is 12, three times six is 24, four times six is...*

Carer: *No, hold on a moment. You got one wrong. Just concentrate. Do it again.*

Child: (Getting very frustrated. Grunts and mutters) *I can't do this! This is too difficult – I can't remember it. I'm no good!*

Carer: *Come on. Don't make a fuss. This is easy...one times six is six, two times six is...*

Child: (Becomes very quiet and subdued. Sits still, eyes downcast)

SCENARIO 3

Child comes home from school looking unhappy.

Carer: *Hello. Oooh, what's up?*

Child: *I had a rotten day. I don't like Angus any more. He went off with my new football at play-time without asking me and he's probably gone and lost it! I hate him!*

Carer: *Has he now? Well, I'll tell you what you need to do. When you go in tomorrow morning, you say to him – if he doesn't give you back your football straight away, I'm going to come and see the teacher. And he won't be getting an invitation to your birthday party next month, will he?*

Child: (Quietly) *Look, it doesn't matter that much, honestly.*

SCENARIO 4

Child comes home cross from school...

Child: (Cross and upset) *Mrs Brown was horrid to me today. She yelled at me, and I felt like crying. But I didn't let anyone see.*

Carer: *What on earth did you do wrong?*

Child: (Bit downcast) *She said I was putting Michael off his work.*

Carer: *What did she say?*

Child: *Can't remember.*

Carer: *Did you get your name on the naughty side of the board?*

Child: *I guess.*

Carer: *Will you get detention?*

Child: *I don't know.*

Carer: *Was that the only time you got in trouble today?*

Child: (Shrugs and turns away)

HANDOUT 9.2

Good listening skills

Attentive listening requires a high level of concentration and energy and an ability both to listen carefully to the overt content of a communication and to tune in to the underlying emotional messages. Listeners need to be able to set aside their own thoughts and priorities and to suspend their judgement. This kind of approach enables the listener to enter into the world of the speaker and to gain understanding of how they perceive events, how they feel and how they think. Some of the qualities that are necessary for this kind of listening are warmth, genuineness and a desire to understand the other person.

Nothing makes children feel more valued and cared for than to be fully listened to.

What does good listening consist of?

- **Listen with full attention**
  Stop what you are doing and focus on the child. You need to be alert to notice all sorts of body language and non-verbal cues as well as focusing on the content. Follow what the child says, going at their pace and respecting whatever it is they feel.

- **Listen with your whole body**
  You may want to face the child and lean forward with an open posture, keeping an appropriate distance. Your attention will signal to the child that you are fully engaged. In some situations you may want to mirror with your own body some aspect of the child's posture or stance. This will convey your understanding and sensitivity.

- **Let the child do the talking**
  Don't interrupt, advise or offer an opinion. Follow the child's thoughts and agenda. Try not to say too much so that you do not disrupt the flow of the child's thinking and expression.

- **Acknowledge feelings**
  We can validate the child's emotional state by our non-verbal gestures or by a word or a sound. We may repeat key words, to show acceptance or to encourage further exploration.

- **Name the feeling**
  It is often helpful if you name the feeling that the child is expressing. This helps the child to clarify what they are thinking and feeling and lets them know that they are understood. Linking words with experiences and feelings builds the child's emotional vocabulary and understanding.

  Child: *I just can't get it right, no matter how many times I try.*

  Carer: *That sounds really discouraging for you. It's not easy to do fractions.*

- **Acknowledge wishes in fantasy**
  Sometimes children express wishes that we cannot fulfil, and yet refusing them may lead to conflict and discord. This may occur when a child tells us that they really don't want to go to bed or that they really must stay up late to watch a new television programme. Instead of trying to reason them out of their wish, it can be helpful to grant in fantasy that which cannot be given in reality. Paradoxically, this may make reality easier to cope with. 'You really wish you didn't have to do this homework. It makes you feel so frustrated'; 'You find it hard going to a new school. You really wish you could stay at home'; 'You really want to go out and

meet your friends but you have to stay in this evening.' This is not to condone the wish but to enable the child to express their feeling more safely.

- **Talk to the feelings and not to the content**
  Sometimes it is not helpful to respond to the literal meaning of a communication. For example, if the child tells you that they are 'going to kill their brother', it is important to distinguish between the feeling and the expressed intention. In the first instance, it will usually be important to acknowledge the feeling and provide space for the child to explore this. When adults can tolerate the expression of strong and difficult feelings they can help children learn how to manage these feelings and find appropriate ways to express them.

  Child: *'I hate Carol. I'm going to smack her one.'*

  Carer: *'You're clearly very angry with Carol. I take that very seriously and I want to know what happened.'*

- **Questions**
  Questions are a useful way of gaining information and moving a conversation on. However, asking too many questions may come across like an interrogation and can inhibit communication.

  Open-ended questions are generally most helpful as they don't have a right or wrong answer and give the child an opportunity to express their views. "What" and "how" are good open-ended questions: 'You look angry – what's happening here?'; 'You're late. What's up?'; 'What you are doing is dangerous. What's going on?'; 'Tell me what happened...'

  "Why" questions, in contrast, are not helpful as a rule because they are likely to be experienced as judgemental. They require the child to understand and take responsibility for their feelings and actions, and many children are not at a stage where they are able to do this.

  Closed questions are ones that have a "yes" or "no" answer. These are best avoided unless you have a very shy or guarded child who won't risk more than a one-word answer. Useful closed questions could be: 'Do you need my help?'; 'Shall I go through that once again?'

- **Reflecting back**
  It is useful to repeat back to the child what you understand them to be saying. This is a kind of mirroring of their thoughts and feelings. Try to be as accurate as you can and name their feelings without judging them as "positive" or "negative".

  'It seems that you...'; 'That sounds as if...'; 'As you see it...'

  All emotions can be accepted and therefore thought about.

HANDOUT 9.3

Scenarios: listening skills

Use the following scenarios with a partner to practise your listening skills. The first line is given in each scenario to start you off.

1 Carer and 10-year-old Jerome

Jerome
It is the weekend. Your brother has been chosen to take part in an inter-school football competition and you have not. You sit flicking your food on the kitchen table and kicking at the chair.

Carer
Use your empathic listening skills to see if Jerome can open up and tell you what is going on for him.

Carer: *You look really fed up.*

2 Carer and eight-year-old Aleesha

Aleesha
You come home from school angry and upset because your best friend went off and played with other girls at break time.

Carer
Try acknowledging and naming Maria's feelings, and use your reflective listening skills to encourage her to tell you what has been happening.

Aleesha: (Angrily) *I'm never going to play with Anita again!*

3 Carer and 11-year-old Rajid

Rajid
You have had a bad day at school and you are cross with your teacher. It feels like everything is going wrong.

Carer
Use your listening skills to encourage Rajid to talk about what has been going on. Relate to the feelings and not the content of what Rajid says.

Rajid: *I hate school. That Mr Bennett is useless. He doesn't know what he is talking about.*

4 Carer and six-year-old Danielle

Danielle
You have homework to do for tomorrow and you hate writing because you find it so hard. You really don't want to do it.

Carer
Try acknowledging Danielle's feelings and see if she is able to talk about it.

Danielle: *This is stupid homework. I don't want to do it! I hate writing.*

5 Carer and seven-year-old Rebecca

Rebecca

You spent ages working on a picture for an art competition and you heard today that it didn't win. You are sad, cross and disappointed.

Carer

Try reflecting back to Rebecca what you think she is feeling and see if you can help her to open up further to you.

Rebecca: *I hate this stupid picture. It's rubbish. I'm useless at drawing.*

HANDOUT 9.4

Home practice: Reflective listening

Try using some of the following skills:	How did you get on?
Give full attention	
Acknowledge and name feelings	
Use open questions	
Reflect feelings and actions	
Be non-judgemental	

SESSION 10: Pulling it together and moving on

TIMETABLE

	Section	Timing	Materials
1.	Starter	**10.00–10.10**	Flip chart
2.	Feedback: listening and paired reading Aims of the session	**10.10–10.55**	Flip chart Slide
3.	Taking paired reading further	**10.55–11.10**	Slides Handout 10.1 *How to progress with paired reading*
4.	Group discussion: motivation – what is it?	**11.10–11.25**	Slide Handout 10.2 *Motivation*
5.	Pairs exercise: exploring motivation	**11.25–11.45**	Slide Flip chart
6.	Small groups exercise: what keeps us motivated?	**11.45–12.15**	Slide Flip chart sheets with pens Handout 10.3 *What keeps us motivated?*
7.	Taking stock: pairs exercise, feedback and discussion	**12.15–12.35**	Handout 10.4 *Taking stock of changes* Flip chart
8.	Closing round	**12.35–12.45**	
9.	Presentation of certificates	**12.45–12.50**	Certificates
10.	Refreshments and goodbyes	**12.50**	Refreshments Music

The last session of any course is likely to leave people with a mix of feelings – a sense of achievement, relief that the hard work is over and sadness at leaving people whom we have got to know and like. There may also be some outstanding issues in carers' minds and questions about where to go from here. You may want to add activities or discussions that address the specific needs of the group in order to create a suitable sense of closure.

This final session should also incorporate a sense of celebration and appreciation of the carers for their hard work and commitment. Make arrangements to present the carers with a certificate of attendance and achievement, consistent with your organisation's policy. You may want to consider asking an appropriate senior member of the department or agency to present these certificates.

Welcome carers as they arrive.

Flip chart, pens
Laptop, CD-ROM with Powerpoint presentation, projector, screen
Certificates
Refreshments
CD player and music CDs

HANDOUTS

Please print off these handouts from the CD-ROM supplied and give each carer a copy of the handouts for today.

10.1 *How to progress with paired reading*
10.2 *Motivation*
10.3 *What keeps us motivated?*
10.4 *Taking stock of changes*
Evaluation form

10 minutes

STARTER

Ask carers to share with the group something they would like to learn, achieve or do in the future.

45 minutes

FEEDBACK

Listening

Find out how carers got on when listening to their children this week. Were they able to use any of the skills discussed in last week's session? Could they tune in to the experiences of the child in any new or significantly different way? How did the children respond?

Paired reading

As this is the last session, it is a good opportunity to get some general feedback on paired reading. Find out what has gone well and anything that has not worked out so well. Write up any outcomes or messages on the flip chart.

Note to trainers: Some carers may have found the paired reading a positive and beneficial experience for the child. Others may have found it more difficult to get the child involved in the reading and they may have needed to think more creatively about how to engage them. After using paired reading for a few weeks, many pairs naturally want to start to vary the ways they read.

Introduce the aims of today's session.

AIMS OF TODAY'S SESSION

- Support carers to continue with and develop paired reading
- Explore "motivation" and what enhances it
- Take stock of what carers have learnt and the impact this has had on them and the children
- Celebrate carers' commitment and achievement

15 minutes

TAKING PAIRED READING FURTHER

Explain to the group that, at this stage, some carers may find they need to adapt the way they are using paired reading with their child. They may decide that the child needs a break from paired reading or that they will use it less frequently. As children progress with their reading, they will want to read more independently.

Use the following slide to explore some of the ways that carers might vary the paired reading experience.

HOW TO PROGRESS WITH PAIRED READING

- "Reading mini-help": child reads alone out loud and adult gives correct word if child makes an error. Child repeats word correctly and continues reading.
- Both adult and child read silently together: they discuss meaning and ask questions at natural break points.
- "Reading solo": adult and child discuss the book. The child goes off to read alone and comes back at intervals to discuss what they have read and clarify anything that they have not understood.

Carers may have their own ideas about how to adapt their paired reading practice. Ask them also to refer to Handout 10.1, *How to progress with paired reading.* The next slide underlines some of the important principles that they should maintain.

REMEMBER TO CONTINUE TO...

- Show interest in your child's reading activity
- Discuss with your child what they are reading and explore meaning
- Give praise and affirmation for reading

Non-critical support for reading maintains self-esteem and motivation

Refer carers to Handout 10.1, *How to progress with paired reading.*

15 minutes

GROUP DISCUSSION

Motivation – what is it?

In this final session we want to spend some time thinking about motivation, as it is a vital component of effective learning – for adults and children alike.

Encourage the group to think about what "motivation" means and to come up with a definition for it.

Note to trainers: The discussion might include some of the following ideas:

Motivation enables us to:

- concentrate and engage with experiences
- direct our attention and achieve our goals through planning and persistence
- resist distractions and keep going in the face of obstacles and setbacks

Motivation

It may be helpful to distinguish between three broad types of motivation.

MOTIVATION
External motivation is based on reward or fear of punishment
Internal motivation involves overcoming short-term pain for longer-term gain
Intrinsic motivation occurs when an activity becomes pleasurable and rewarding in itself

---

Explain to the group that these ideas can be related to the process of learning to read. In the early stages, the child will often be driven by external factors, for example, the promise of praise from their carer, a star in their book or fear of ridicule from peers. As they progress, they will become more internally motivated and they may want to read so that they can follow instructions or find information. Once their reading skills are established, they may discover that reading is an enjoyable and rewarding activity in itself. Some activities may involve a combination of different types of motivation. Handout 10.2, *Motivation,* offers more details.

20 minutes

PAIRS EXERCISE

Exploring motivation

Explain to the group that motivation is a complex concept. In order to understand it more fully, we are going to explore some of the wide range of factors that affect our motivation.

Ask carers to look at the list of challenges on the following slide and add to this with examples of challenges that they have personally taken on. Write these on the flip chart.

CHALLENGES I HAVE TAKEN ON...

Going to the gym
Attending evening classes
Doing a DIY project
Learning how to use the computer
Training for a marathon
Organising a party for a friend
Learning to drive
Climbing a mountain
Going on a diet

In pairs, ask carers to:

- select a specific challenge that they have undertaken
- reflect on the reasons that persuaded or motivated them to pursue this

Encourage carers to think about the thoughts, beliefs and feelings that influenced their motivation, and identify factors in the environment that supported them.

Take feedback from the pairs and write up any learning points on the flip chart.

Factors might include:

- time
- aptitude
- fun
- sense of achievable challenge
- personal temperament
- competition
- need/desperation
- belief in the value of an activity
- use and relevance of challenge
- a means to an end (e.g. learning to use the computer in order to support child with learning or to use email to communicate with friends)
- encouragement from others
- joint endeavour

30 minutes

SMALL GROUPS EXERCISE

What keeps us motivated?

Divide the carers into two groups. Display the slide below.

WHAT KEEPS US MOTIVATED?

Using the image on the slide, ask the carers to think about the different factors that affect motivation and to write down their ideas under the five different headings on a flip chart sheet.

FACTORS AFFECTING MOTIVATION

Environment: factors which support motivation, including behaviour and attitudes of others
Skills: specific and general
Personal factors: temperament, mood and beliefs about self
Social and emotional skills
Task: what are the qualities of the task that make it motivating?

They should start by thinking about the kinds of factors in the environment that might support motivation and then move on to consider skills, personal factors and specific social and emotional skills. Finally, they should consider the qualities of the task itself that may make it more or less motivating.

Ask the groups to feed back their thoughts.

Refer carers to Handout 10.3, *What keeps us motivated?* for further ideas.

Note to trainers: This exercise should draw on many of the skills and themes that have been explored in the course of the training programme. Some of the factors affecting motivation in a child are beyond the control of the carer. However, there are many significant factors in the home environment and in the way carers communicate and relate to the children in their care that can have a substantial and lasting impact on children's motivation and achievements.

20 minutes

TAKING STOCK

Explain to the group that they are now going to reflect on their own learning during the course of the training programme and think about the impact that this may have had on their attitudes to learning and on their behaviour. They are also going to consider any changes in their children's attitudes and behaviour and their relationship with each other.

PAIRS EXERCISE

Taking stock

Using Handout 10.4, *Taking stock of changes*, as a starting point, ask carers to share their thoughts with a partner.

Feedback

In the large group, ask each carer to name one positive change or achievement that has taken place for them during the course of training, and one positive change or achievement that has taken place for the child. Give plenty of specific praise for the work carers have done, whether this is for progress they have made or for effort they have put in. Write the specific achievements, gains and changes on the flip chart so that there is a sense of celebration and acknowledgement of what has been done.

Open discussion

You may want to allow an opportunity now for carers to raise any outstanding issues that they wish to, and for you to get any further feedback on the training that would be helpful to you.

10 minutes

CLOSING ROUND

Ask carers in turn to share two things with the group. Ask them to say one thing that they have appreciated about being together in the group. Then encourage them to share what is most important for them at the present time to work on with their child.

5 minutes

PRESENTATION OF CERTIFICATES

REFRESHMENTS

Following the presentation, refreshments should be served with appropriate music and other arrangements to celebrate the end of the course.

HANDOUT 10.1

How to progress with paired reading

After a few weeks, you and your child may be happy to continue with paired reading in the same way, or you may feel the need to adapt the way you are reading together.

- You may want to have a break from paired reading and then perhaps start again later
- You may want to continue but possibly less frequently

Other alternatives are:

1) **"Reading mini-help":** child reads aloud, alone, and adult gives correct word if the child makes an error. Child repeats word correctly and continues reading alone.
2) **Reading silently:** both adult and child read page silently at the same time. They discuss the meaning and ask questions at natural break points.
3) **Reading solo:** adult and child discuss book. The child reads silently on their own. The child comes to talk with the adult at natural break points to discuss and ask questions. If necessary, you can agree when the next natural break might occur so that the child does not go on too long.

Remember:

You will probably still need to read together with very hard books.

GIVE LOTS OF PRAISE AT EVERY STAGE!!

HANDOUT 10.2

Motivation

Motivation may be defined as: what prompts us to engage with experiences and set goals for the future, and to achieve this through planning and persistence, in the face of boredom, obstacles and setbacks.

It enables us to concentrate, direct our attention and resist distractions.

There are different aspects of motivation.

- **External motivation:** this operates when we do something for reward, like completing a chore for payment, or when we do something to avoid a punishment, such as doing homework to avoid detention.
- **Internal motivation:** this refers to our personal ability to overcome short-term "pain" for the sake of long-term "gain". An example of this would be studying hard in order to get a qualification, or doing exercises in order to lose weight or get fit.
- **Intrinsic motivation:** this occurs when an activity is, or becomes, pleasurable in its own right. This could be something like eating chocolate, reading a book or playing a musical instrument.

We need motivation in order to work towards future goals. If a child wants to get into a football team, they will have to commit themselves to practise even when they don't feel like it and they may need to train for weeks or months before they get a chance of being chosen. This involves both the control of impulses and the delay of gratification.

Motivation is also strengthened by other general skills, such as:

- self-awareness and the ability to manage feelings
- the ability to recognise strengths and limitations
- strategies for managing disappointment and setbacks
- strategies for promoting positive thinking and positive emotional states

Motivation is affected by the nature of the task.

Is the task interesting, fun, rewarding, relevant, too hard or too easy? Children can easily become disinterested and de-motivated if learning is not stimulating, relevant and targeted at an appropriate ability level.

Motivation is affected by our beliefs.

- Do we think the task is achievable?
- Do we believe we have the ability to fulfil the task?
- What do we believe about success and failure?
- Do we feel responsible for our goals and actions?
- Do we have a pessimistic or an optimistic attitude?

Locus of control: Some children believe that the factors relating to success lie within their control, for example, that they can achieve success through hard work and practice. This is called an "internal locus of control". Others believe that success depends on external factors like luck, fate or perhaps the actions or influence of other people. This is known as an "external locus of control".

Environment: Motivation and resilience are greatly affected by context. Children are more likely to develop good motivation when they receive praise and affirmation, when they are encouraged to think positively, and when their mistakes are seen as part of the learning process.

HANDOUT 10.3

What keeps us motivated?

GOAL

Environment

Supportive ethos and relationships
Praise and recognition
Safe to make mistakes
Belief of others
Feedback

Skills

Specific:
Skills, aptitudes, behaviours
Learning style

General:
Problem solving
Organisational
Anticipating obstacles
Self awareness: knowing strengths and weaknesses

Personal factors

Temperament:
Energetic, good concentration, etc

Belief in self:
Positive thoughts and attitudes. Good self-esteem

Emotional state:
Positive, optimistic

Social and emotional skills

Persistence:
Managing feelings
Delaying gratification
Resisting distraction
Managing boredom

Resilience:
Positive beliefs
Tolerating mistakes
Overcoming setbacks
Keeping focus on big picture

TASK

Relevant?
Fun?
Interesting?
Too hard?
Too easy?
Does it fit child's skills/aptitudes?
Does child "own" the task?
Is it rewarding?

HANDOUT 10.4

Taking stock of changes

Is my behaviour different in any way?

Is my child responding to any changes in me or in the home environment?

Has my child's behaviour changed for the better in any way?

Is there anything that I would like to be more confident in dealing with?

References

Barnardo's (2006) *Failed by the System: The views of young care leavers on their educational experience*, London: Barnardo's, available at: www.barnardos.org.uk/failed_by_the_system_report.pdf

DH and DfES (2000) *Guidance on the Education of Children and Young People in Public Care*, London: DH and DfES

Evangelou M and Sylva K (2003) *The Effects of the Peers Early Education Partnership (PEEP) on Children's Developmental Progress*, DfES Research Report RB489, London: DfES

Jackson S and Martin PY (1998) 'Surviving the care system: education and resilience', *Journal of Adolescence*, 21:5, pp 569–583

Morris E and Casey J (2006) *Developing Emotionally Literate Staff: A practical guide*, London: Paul Chapman

Nolte DL (1972) *Children Learn what they Live*, available at: www.empowermentresources.com/info2/childrenlearn-long_version.html

Ritchie A (2003) *Care to Learn? The educational experiences of children and young people who are looked after*, London: Save the Children

Social Exclusion Unit (2003) *A Better Education for Children in Care*, London: Social Exclusion Unit

Further reading

Bhabra S, Ghate D and Brazier, L (2002) *Raising the Educational Attainment of Children in Care*, Consultation Analysis for the Social Exclusion Unit, London: SEU, Cabinet Office

Brooks G (2002) *What Works for Children with Literacy Difficulties? The Effectiveness of Intervention Scheme*, DfES Research Report No 380, London: DfES

Cairns K and Stanway C (2004) *Learn the Child: Helping looked after children to learn*, London: BAAF

Desforges C and Abouchaar A (2003) *The Impact of Parental Involvement, Parental Support and Family Education on Pupil Achievements and Adjustment: A Literature Review*, DfES Research Report No 433, London: DfES

DfES (2003) *Involving Parents, Raising Achievement: Materials for schools*, London: DfES

DfES and DfEE (2001) *Promoting Children's Mental Health within Early Years and School Settings*, London: DfES and DfEE

Dixon B (2008) *Education: A carer's handbook*, London: National Teaching and Advisory Service

Fletcher-Campbell F (1997) *The Education of Children Who Are Looked After*, Slough: National Foundation for Educational Research (NFER)

Geddes H (2006) *Attachment in the Classroom: The links between children's early experience, emotional well-being and performance in school*, London: Worth Publishing

Golding K (2006) *Thinking Psychologically about Children who are Looked After and Adopted*, Chichester: John Wiley and Sons

Harker R, Dobel-Ober D, Berridge D and Sinclair R (2004) *Taking Care of Education: An evaluation of the education of looked after children*, London: National Children's Bureau

Hunt C and Mountford A (2003) *The Parenting Puzzle*, Oxford: The Family Links Nurturing Programme

Jackson S and McParlin P (2006) 'The education of children in care', *The Psychologist*, 19:2, pp 90–93

Killick S (2006) *Emotional Literacy at the Heart of the School Ethos*, London: Sage Publications

Lucas B and Smith A (2002) *Help your Child to Succeed: The essential guide for parents*, Stafford: Network Educational Press Ltd

Martin PY and Jackson S (2002) 'Educational success for children in public care: advice from a group of high achievers', *Child and Family Social Work*, 7, pp 121–130

National Literacy Trust (2001) *Parental Involvement and Literacy Achievement*, Consultation Paper, London: National Literacy Trust

Nutbrown C, Hannon P and Morgan A (2005) *Early Literacy Work with Families: Policy, practice and research*, London: Sage Publications

Rees S and Savitsky F (2001) *Helping my Child with Reading and Writing*, London: South Bank University, London Language and Literacy Unit

SEAL materials, available at: http://nationalstrategies.standards.dcsf.gov.uk/primary/behaviourattendanceandseal/primaryseal

Sinclair R (1998) *The Education of Children in Need*, London: National Children's Bureau

Stannard P (2002) *Think Good and Feel Good*, Chichester: John Wiley and Sons

Supporting SEAL (Social and Emotional Aspects of Learning) (2008) *The Parent Pack*, Bristol: Futurelink Publishing

Topping KJ (2001) *Thinking Reading Writing: A practical guide to paired learning with peers, parents and volunteers*, New York and London: Continuum International, available at: www.dundee.ac.uk/eswce/research/projects/trw/

Webster-Stratton C (1999) *How to Promote Children's Social and Emotional Competence*, London: Paul Chapman Publishers Ltd

Wheal A (1998) *The RHP Companion to Foster Care*, Lyme Regis: Russell House Publishing

Whitehouse E and Pudney W (1996) *A Volcano in my Tummy: Helping children to handle anger*, Gabriola Island, BC, Canada: New Society Publishers

Wolfendale S and Bryans T (2004) *Evaluation of the Looking After Literacy Project in Kent for Children in Public Care*, London: University of East London

Wolfendale S and Topping K (1996) *Family Involvement in Literacy*, London: Cassell

Wray D (1996) 'Teaching literacy: the foundations of good practice', *Education 3 to 13*, 27:1, pp 53–59

The Who Cares? Trust (2003) *Education Matters For Everyone Working with Children in Public Care*, London: The Who Cares? Trust